C Language
/* & C++ */

A quick and easy course

Cacildo Marques

ARTE DE CAPA

Cacildo Marques

Episteme-Ed-Butantan

C Language
/* & C++ */

A quick and easy course

Cacildo Marques

Marques, Cacildo

C LANGUAGE /* & C++ */: A quick and easy course / Cacildo

Marques -- São Paulo: Amazon Sistema CreateSpace, 2016.

ISBN 978-1530254842

1. C (Linguagem de programação para computadores) I. Marques,
Cacildo II. Título

CDD-005.1

Fathers – and mothers – of C language

Blaise Pascal (1623-1662)
Calculator

Gottlob Wilhelm Leibniz (1646-1716)
Binary arithmetic

Ada Byron (1815-1851)
Programming

Alan Turing (1912-1954)
Paper computer

Alonzo Church (1903-1995)
Programming language

Konrad Zuse (1910-1995)
Binary computer

Grace Murray Hopper (1906-1992)
Compiler

Denis M. Ritchie (1941-2011)
C language

PREFACE

Nobody learns a serious matter using a single book. If in class the teacher adopts a book that the student uses, and that seems enough for learning, this sufficiency is because the teacher plays the role of a second book, a talking book, elaborating in real time.

So if this is the first book of programming language for the reader, there is not by the author claim to teach you the C language without the aid of any other source. However, once what is presented here covers virtually all of the C resources, it is enough the player, in case of any doubt, to refer to the Internet, asking for examples of the topic in question. The great advantage of having a book in your hands is the organized presentation of the subject in didactic order, from easy to difficult, from usual to sporadic.

You learn a programming language from existing programs, either using them as a model, or making changes and adaptations in them. If the reader follows the proposal of this material without skipping sections, but experiencing playback programs and mini-programs here presented, in the order given, preferably typing word for word, and doing the exercises at the end of the study, that is, completing the reading and application of the projects presented, he will be ready to create his own programs, with content domain. If you also want to learn by heart every reserved word of the original C language, this will be a good acquisition, since in other languages the number of these words is always greater.

You must be very careful when entering the codes. For the computer, half a word is not enough. The lack of a comma, the exchange of a comma by a semi-colon, a quotation mark typed with some special formatting, the absence of a directive or statement, all that disables the program. The first notice, in the order of lines and hits presented in the feedback of a faulty program, is the relevant information. One should not spend time with the following lines error codes because they are affected by the first error in the order of execution. For example, if the word "main" is typed capitalized, they will come several error messages after the warning on that word, but the priority is to fix this first failure, so that the following messages, if they persist, make sense.

In the first year of university, programming teachers do not consider the student as an entry level apprentice, but see him at least as an individual with average preparation, when they do not see him as expert, just as in music colleges. In the case of Exact Sciences and Engineering colleges, it is difficult to know the origin of so high expectations, but the lesson is that the student has to learn to run behind his demands, forgetting the high school time, where teachers demanded short tasks and still tolerated delays. The fact is that the first programs ordered as exercises are already hearty works, in a whole page or more. If you are that situation, you can start practicing here with this book and in your own computer

The novice programmer eventually learns a new language, used to talk to the machine, but also to talk to other developers. While mastering a language, the citizen puts the machine to obey his orders, comfortably, unlike what occurs when he who receives orders to accomplish is a being of flesh and blood, once you cannot know what this individual has in mind when he answers the charge. What we should not forget is the importance of interaction with our peers, naturally, without industrial interfaces. With this in mind, we can give ourselves to learning programming, which is based on C and C++ languages, although there are several previous languages. Enjoy!

CONTENTS

Entry and exit by keyboard and video

The *iostream.h*-header file C++

System-level input and output

Recursion

Quick ordering

Selective sorting

Binary search

Divide and conquer

Chapter 0

INTRODUCTION - The C language

At the Bell Laboratories of AT & T in the United States, Ken Thompson used to utilize a language called "B", which he created from another language developed by Martin Richards in Cambridge, MA, BCPL programming language (*Basic Combined Programming Language*), derived from Algol 60. From the B language, Dennis M. Ritchie (1941-2011) created in 1972 a revolutionary new language, which he called C. When Ken Thompson then wrote the UNIX operating system, at the same AT & T, chose to do it with the C language, and no longer with the *assembly* language, as expected. The basic book of C has been written by Dennis M. Ritchie and Brian W. Kernighan under the name of *The C Programming Language* (Prentice Hall, 1978).

Over time, C became the preferred language of system developers and with it they wrote things like dBASE III, Windows and the computer graphics sequences of "Return of the Jedi."

Human language

The main packages sold in the market are made in C. This is because it was the fastest language processing among high-level languages, because of its constitution almost stenographic and its compatibility with the *assembly* language. We called "high-level language" that language whose codes are similar to human language and the first steps in its development were given in 1943, in Berlin, with the *plankalkül*, by civil engineer Konrad Zuse. Once completed his university degree in 1935, he, as a Ford's German subsidiary engineer, began to implement the construction of the first binary computer in the history, which he called Z1. Without participation of the Nazi government, which has denied support, he had to rely on financing from merchants and friends. This first machine failed to work, so he created the successor Z2 and Z3, this in 1941, already with some funding from the government, pressured by war needs. For the Z3 is that Zuse developed the *plankalkül*, but that machine did not performed conditional jumps (the IF statement) and the *plankalkül* was not much more advanced than what would be the *assembly* language, although it represented a new step related to the purely formal *lambda calculus* system, of Alonzo Church, of 1936. The purpose of Church was to develop a language that was compatible with the Turing machine (the famous "paper computer"). By the end of 1943 an air raid on Berlin destroyed those machines, but Zuse had already started the construction of the Z4. The record of its patents came to IBM's hands in 1946, but the completion of the Z4 in Germany only has occurred in 1949.

Also in 1943 in Pennsylvania, USA, John Von Neumann and his team developed, based on ideas of Alan Turing, of whom Neumann was advisor in Princeton, the ENIAC Coding System, to the computer that he were building. In 1946, with the machine already in operation, Neumann developed with Richard Clippinger a more substantial language, the *Short Code*.

In 1952, Lieutenant Grace Murray Hopper, mathematics professor at Harvard University, presented his language *A-0* with the first compiler in the history, as a refinement of the *Short Code*, and later she created also more advanced codes such as languages

Arith-Matic (1954) and *Flow-Matic* (1955), using human words of English. In 1952 the *Speedcoding*, of John W. Backus, also appeared, as predecessor of the *Fortran* (formula translator) language, which was conceived in 1954 and launched commercially in 1957. Since then, many high-level languages have been developed in universities and industry.

The languages closest of the machine "understanding", written in numeric code, such as *ARC Assembly*, are called machine languages and are considered low-level languages. The faster they are in processing, the less readable they are by the human element, for giving heed to the restrictions of the machine.

Chronology of languages

1936: Lambda Calculus
1943: Plankalkul
1943: ENIAC Coding System
1946: ENIAC Short Code
1947: ARC Assembly
1952: A-0
1955: Flow-Matic
1957: Fortran
1958: Algol 58, APT
1959: Lisp
1960: Algol 60, Cobol
1962: Snobol
1964: Basic, PL/I
1965: Algol W
1967: BCPL
1968: Algol 68, Logo
1969: B, APL
1970: Pascal
1971: Forth

1972: C, Prolog, SQL
1976: Modula
1978: Visicalc, Matlab, C Shell
1979: Ada
1980: Smaltalk
1981: Modula-2
1983: Objective-C
1984: dBASE III
1985: Clipper, Paradox
1987: Perl, Mathematica
1988: C++
1991: GNU E, Python, HTML, Visual Basic
1993: R
1995: Delphi, Java, PHP, Ruby, Javascript
1996: CSS
2000: C#, D
2001: Visual Basic .NET
2004: Groovy
2009: Go
2012: Julia
2014: Swift

More profitable (concerning to wage):

1. Ruby
2. Objective-C
3. Python
4. Java
5. C++

6. Javascript
7. C
8. R
9. C#
10. Visual Basic .NET

Popularity of languages in 2016, by the TIOBE Index
(www.tiobe.com/index.php/tiobe_index):

1. Java	11. Perl
2. C	12. Delphi
3. C++	13. Visual Basic
4. C#	14. Swift
5. Python	15. Matlab
6. PHP	16. Pascal
7. Visual Basic .NET	17. Groovy
8. Javascript	18. Objective-C
9. Assembly	19. R
10. Ruby	20. PL

Remark: In January 2015 the first place in popularity was C, which lost his position to Java, but Java and JavaScript languages are derived from C, the latter having basically the same syntax. CSS, HTML and SQL are not Turing-complete languages (Turing-complete language is one that has computational power equivalent to the Turing machine, i. e., the language and the universal Turing machine can emulate each other).

CHAPTER 1

THE COMPILER

The high-level languages are classified into compiled and interpreted. A program written in interpreted language is executed through the reading line by line made by the processor. Whereas a program in compiled language runs in a comprehensive manner by the processor, which then works much faster.

The first presentation written and debugged of a program on the screen is called a "source program" and in this state the program is executed if the programming code is an interpreted language. If, instead, we are working with a compiled language, so we need to pass the source program for the compiling phase, which turns it into object program and assign it a name that usually has the .OBJ extension, as in CONTROL.OBJ. The program that performs this process is called a compiler, which exists in different versions, either for C language, C++, Clipper, Delphi, Visual Basic, or for many other codes.

The compilation phase, however, is not the final step in developing a program. The program with .OBJ extension, called object program, to become executable must go through the process of link-editing, getting an extension as .EXE, .DLL, .COM, etc.

The C language features compiler, and not an interpreter, being therefore a language that allows the creation of very fast execution programs. A source program in C has the .CPP (C++ or C Plus Plus) or simply .C extensions.

Structured languages

One of the elements that facilitate the work of the compiler in C is that this language favors writing structured programs, i. e., programs designed in modules that compose or mating themselves, allowing to avoid the use of deviations given by the *goto* statement, although such an instruction still takes part of the language.

The basic quality criterion for the development of programs is the runtime economy and memory usage of the machine. Given two versions of a program, the preferred is the one that best meets that criterion and, therefore, a program written in a structured form earns points, unless it wastes time and memory for nothing.

Once the source program is typed it should be saved to a file format, having received thus a name that should be one to eight characters, starting by letter or dash (underscore: "_") and followed by letters, indents or numbers. Its extension should be .C to any C compiler and may be .CPP in the case of C++ compilers.

C++ compilers provide appropriate environments for programming, organized in windows and buttons, where you can enter, compile, link-edit and run the program, using for these three last steps the keyboard or only the mouse. We can reproduce programs snippets in C++ environment by the technique of marking (highlighting) the text, transporting it to the clipboard - Ctrl + Ins keys - and, hence, tossing it in C++ screen - Shift + Ins keys - when then it must be unmarked - Ctrl + KH keys.

The environment of Borland Turbo C++ compiler has received at factory the name of Integrated Development Environment (IDE) and is part of the directory named BIN. To enter this directory, type, from the DOS prompt, cd \TurboC\BIN and key to enter. Being in the directory, access to the environment is obtained by typing BC, Enter, this being just one of the ways to get to the Turbo C++

environment. Obviously, if at the time of starting (boot) the AUTOEXEC.BAT file contains the 'Path' the words "C:\TurboC\BIN;", it is enough to key BC and Enter on any directory prompt, either at the root, the Windows Run or a strange directory, to immediately enter the C++ environment. To activate any of the BC Environment window just press F10 and arrows (¬, ¯, ®). In C++ compilers for other brands, proceed in a similar manner, adapting the words. By the way, Microsoft activates windows with Alt.

Get Borland TurboC++ 3.0 on: http://winworldpc.com (decompress with 7z and then *WinImage*)

Compilation

Nothing prevents to operate, however, in the old way, by entering the .C extension program in any word processor, or in the DOS itself, and by making the compilation and link-editing right there at the operating system prompt. A program called, for example, TEST1.C, recorded in the current directory, can be compiled by typing C TEST1.C, CL TEST1.C, or TC TEST1.C, depending on whether the call to your compiler is C, CL or CT, or even another as EC, CC, BCC or LC. Borland TurboC++ 3.0 compiler uses the TCC command to work on the command line. So if TEST1.C is in the *TurboC**Progs* folder, since we are in *TurboC**bin*, just do TCC *TurboC**Progs*\TEST1.C for the program to compile the file, and to generate in the current directory the file TEST1.EXE. Now writing on the command line the TEST1 name, it starts running.

The reader can also download the GNU compiler, GCC, the Gnu Compiler Collection, for Windows or Linux. With it, the compilation is done from the command prompt. If it is installed in Mingw folder, you should go to the Bin subdirectory, by typing CD *Mingw**bin*. If your software sources are stored in *Mingw**Programs* folder, and there, for example, Newtest.c program is recorded, to compile it you should type, being in the bin folder: *gcc \mingw\programs\ Newtest.c -o Newtest*

Pressing Enter, if the program is correct, with the necessary directives (it must have been started with at least *#include <stdio.h>*), the word NEWTEST after -o code takes the compiler to create the inside the Bin folder the Novotest.exe program. This name, entered after -o, could have been changed, because there is no need to match the name of the source program. It could have been IHaveHit to generate the IHaveHit.exe program.

C program

To write a program in C language we need to use variables, statements, reserved words of the language and functions.

Functions can be user-defined in the program itself or on previously recorded files, or can be called of the *standard library*, which always accompanies C. This *standard library* is, after all, a library of libraries, a sort of necessary appendix to the language, and access to it is obtained with the use of directives *#include <...>* at the beginning of the program. Let's look at a small example:

Example-program #1

```
/* Program "Eachname.cpp" */
#include <stdio.h>

void main(void)
{
    char m[80];
    printf("\n Type your name: ");
    gets(m); puts(m);
    printf("\n Your name is: \n %s",m);
}
```

At the example-program above, the reserved words are *char* and *void*. The used functions are *main()*, *printf()*, *gets()* and *puts()*, which belong to the *stdio.h* library (this comes from "standard input-output"). The *char* and *void* words are types of declarations for variables or functions. The word *void* is optional in the updated versions of C and is, or was, used only to occupy the space of one non-existent type (variable), so that the programmer did not lose the habit of declaring variables. The expression '%s' in *printf()* means "substitute the variable string for its content". Whereas '% .15s' indicates that the impression will be occur only at the first fifteen touches. If we write '% .8s', the impression will go only until the eighth character.

This first example is a slightly more loaded presentation of the classis mini-program "Hello, World", published by Ritchie and Kernighan in his 1978 book on the C language:

```
main(){
     printf("Hello World\n"); return 0;}
```

To see the result

If you are programming in the own "environment" of C++, after pressing F10 (or Alt) and arrows to highlight Run menu, down arrow to open the window and finally Run to compile, link-edit and run the program, you must open the *Window* tab, take down arrow and press Enter in *Output*, to see the DOS prompt screen. With the cursor arrows you can scroll the screen vertically or horizontally. The active window will be the Output. To reactivate the window script, press Close, which closes Output, the current window. To record the program, click Save As on the File menu and type the name, up to eight characters, baptizing it. Press Enter.

In the IDE from Borland, the reader can see the output screen, which is the DOS command line, simply by typing Alt + F5.

Exercises

1) Make a program that prints the name and surnames of the programmer, one on each line ('\n' is the line changing of the impression), using *printf()* on each name or, if you can and like, once.

2) Make a program that receives a phrase from the keyboard and print it three times: one from the beginning of the line, another with some blanks left (just leave spaces in the formatting before '%s') and another only with the first twelve characters. To do this, repeat the *printf()*. Caution: declaring *char m*[80] indicates that the vector *m* can receive a line of a maximum of 79 characters. The last character, the eightieth there, is the null character, which is reserved.

CHAPTER 2

RESERVED WORDS AND OTHER CODES

For the choice of variables in a program is necessary to avoid using any of the reserved words of the language, once this would lead to an error message and interrupt the execution.

In C there is a very small number of reserved words since functions are not part of this group, whereas they are belonging to the standard library and not to the body language. In C, the I/O mechanisms (*input/output*) are part of the set of library functions, contrary to what occurs with other languages.

The C language should not be the first programming code to any student, because after get used to the short way to write a statement on it, it is difficult to accept the discursive style of other high-level languages. But it is the most important language. So to prevent the reader who does not work with another language comes to develop such a barrier, this book attempts to draw comparisons with Pascal, whenever it is convenient. At this point, it should be said that while in Pascal external modules to the main program are *procedures*, much more than functions, in C these modules are all handled as functions, with exception to the rule only in definitions of parameterized variables. And also in comparison with Pascal, it should be noted that braces, {...}, modules bounding in C, in Pascal have the corresponding form *begin ... end.* The main program, that in Pascal has just to come wrapped in these two words, has in C the opening function *main()*, without which nothing works in the language.

Reserved words in C, defined by ANSI (*American National Standards Institute*), are these 32, as follows:

auto	double	int	struct
break	else	long	switch
case	enum	register	typedef
char	extern	return	union
const	float	Short	unsigned
continue	for	signed	void
default	goto	sizeof	volatile
do	if	static	white

The reader will see that only 13 of these words have not role of type modifiers. They are as follows: *break, case, continue, default, do, else, for, goto, if, return, sizeof, switch* and *while*.

Remark: In the original language, from Kernighan and Ritchie, there were not the words *const, enum, signed, void* and *volatile*, adopted by ANSI. And there was a word that was never implemented: *entry*.

More words

In addition to the 32 reserved words defined by ANSI, the Microsoft C compiler (MSC) also uses the words *_asm, cdecl, far, fortran, huge, near* and *pascal*. The increases in Turbo C to ANSI are: *asm, cdecl, _cs, _de, _es, far, huge, interrupt, near, pascal* and *_ss*.

The word *asm*, or *_asm*, serves to introduce the C programming an *Assembly* routine, which may require its own directive, as *#pragma inline*. The routine can be as follows:

```
asm {
    push es
    pop es
}
```

The word *cdecl* tells the compiler that in the call of functions of other languages the reading of parameters should be done in the normal order of C, from right to left, and not in the order of the source language. The word *far* tells the processor that the modified pointer uses 32 bits instead of 16. The modifiers *fortran* and *pascal* warn the compiler that the passing of function parameters must be made in the order used for those languages (left to right). The modifier *huge* makes the pointer modified by it necessarily to use 32 bits.

The word *interrupt* is a modifier that identifies a function as an interrupt routine. The *near* pointer is a modifier function that tells the compiler to use 16 bits. The modifiers *_cs, _ds, _es* and *_es* are pointers that tell the compiler to use the pointed segments. In Borland Turbo C++, registrars can be called directly through *_AH, _AL, _BH*, etc.

Arithmetical operators

In decreasing order of precedence, the arithmetical operators in C are as follows:

Operator   Role

-	unary (signal)
+	unary (signal)
++	unary (increment)
--	unary (decrement)
*	multiplicative (multiplication)
/	multiplicative (division)
%	multiplicative (remainder of the division)
+	additive (sum)
-	additive (subtraction)

Remark: The powering operation will be obtained by the *pow()* function, of the header file *math.h*.

Boolean operators

The following are the logical, or Boolean, operators in C:

Operator   Role

|	unary (*not*)
&&	binary (*and*)
||	binary (*or*)

Relational operators and others

Besides the above operators, C language also has the table below, presented in descending order of precedence:

Operator   Role

( )	belonging (function argument)
[]	belonging (array index)
.	belonging (access structure)
->	belonging (reference for 'pointer')
~	unary (complementary one)
*	unary (the 'pointer' indicator)
&	unary (address)
sizeof	unary (size baites)
(type)	type of change (variables)
<<	bitwise (shift left)
>>	bitwise (shift right)
<	relational (less than)
>	relational (greater than)
<=	relational (or less)
>=	relational (or greater)

= =	relational (comparative equality)
!=	relational (not equal)
&	bitwise (bitwise AND)
|	bitwise (bitwise OR)
^	bitwise (bitwise XOR)
?...:	conditional ternary (condition)
=	assignment (equality)
*=	assignment (iterative multiplication)
/=	assignment (iterative division)
%=	assignment (iterative remainder)
+=	assignment (iterative addition)
-=	assignment (iterative subtraction)
<<=	assignment (iterative shift-left)
>>=	assignment (shift-right iterative)
&=	assignment (iterative intersection)
^=	assignment (iterative or exclusive)
|=	assignment (inclusive or iterative)
,	sequencing (in instructions)

The following program creates and uses the function named Symb(), whose role is simply to print a sequence of graphic characters from the ASCII table (*American Standard Code for International Interchange*):

 Example-program #2

```
/* Program "Symbol.cpp" */
#include <stdio.h>

void Symb( )
    {
        printf("\n\n *I©¦ _ _ _ ¦©I* \n");
    }
main( )
    {
        Symb();
        printf("\n\n It works actually!\n");
    }
```

To put on the screen the graphic symbols of the print line of the Symb() function, you must press the Alt key and type on the numeric keypad, with 'num-lock' on, the ASCII number of these symbols.

After releasing the Alt key, the symbol corresponding to the number will be on the screen. The table contains the codes numbered from zero to 1023 (four pages of 256 positions). Here are some of them for the reader to choose:

Alt+ 15 = ¤	Alt+ 176= »	Alt+225 = ß
Alt+ 157=Ø	Alt+ 183=À	Alt+231 = þ
Alt+ 172=¼	Alt+ 185 = ¦	Alt+234 =Û
Alt+ 174= «	Alt+190 = ¥	Alt+241 = ±

In the second line of the program it is one of the processor directives, the *#include* statement. These directives provide access to standard library functions that the program needs to use. Before, in the first line, there is an expression wrapped in the symbols "/ *"

and "* /". It is the code of comments in C, equivalent to the pair "(*" and "*)" in Pascal. Whatever is between "/ *" and "* /" will be ignored by the processor, for purposes of the program execution, even if the opening and closing of the comment are in different lines, such as, for example, in:

/ * This is to show
how a comment in C works. * /

In line 4 (line 3 is blank) it is the declaration of the function Symb(), user-defined function, in this case, this author. If it returned a character, it would be "*char* Symb()", if it returned an integer number, it would be "*int* Symb()", and so on. As it does not produce any value, but just does print a set of symbols, the reserved word used in the statement was *void*. These *void* type functions would be *procedures*, instead functions, in languages such as Pascal or clipper.

In the argument of the *printf()* function, in line 6, we have after quotes the code '\n \n'. Each format '\n' in this function tells the processor that the printer will skip to the next line. The letter 'f' in *printf()* means 'formatted'. It is the formatted printing function.

Inside the *main()* function, we have, on lines 10 and 11, the call to two functions, Symb() and *printf()*. Each is terminated by a semicolon, which is the way it ends any instructions written in C and Pascal. Note the reader that the declarations (constants, functions or directives) do not end with semi-colon, and the same happens with the comment line closure. User-defined functions, as is the case with Symb(), are usually written with initial capital, not to be confused with the standard library functions.

Some remarks

Capital letters. In C language, uppercase and lowercase letters are distinct codes. Thus, a reserved word can be used as a variable if it is written in capital letters, as in Auto (the reserved word is *auto*).

Error messages. In most cases, the error message in the program compilation is far from pointing out the true diagnosis of the problem. With experience, the programmer will be familiarized with the interpretation of these messages. In other situations, the error is in earlier passages to the line really indicated by the cursor.

Indentation. The indentation, jagged writing of program lines, with some getting more right than others, does not say almost anything to the machine, but it is an aesthetic organization aiming the reading by the programmer himself or by a third party. It is important, for example, the opening brace is coupled with its closure. For this, the other elements are indented.

Care. In addition to the distinction between zero (0) and the letter 'O', what is a big problem for those starting in Computer Science, In C should be taken care also not to mix the comparative equality ("= =") with assignment ("="). The symbol "=" is used to store in the variable on the left the contents of the expression to the right, as at x = 3*5; or y = *cos*(3.14);. Whereas the symbol "= =" is used only for conditions that have always surrounded by parentheses, as we shall see later in the study of the *if-else*, *while* and *do-while* commands. Another care that should be taken refers to the ergonomic aspect. It is the use of the mouse. It's not convenient trigger it always with the index finger, which is not prepared for this overload. If the user wants to click it always with the same finger, then use the thumb, which is much more appropriate for this. Anyway, there are not any cases of tendonitis in typists who know divide the work of the index finger with other fingers. It is absolutely reckless to type only with your index fingers. If the player does not practice typing, buy a little program training - there are many in the software shops - and stick to it for a few weeks.

Exercises

1) Write a program that prints three short sentences, using a *printf()* for each.

2) Make a program in which it is created, then used inside the

main(), one function named Beep(), declared *void* Beep(), whose role will be to give a whistle whenever called. A whistle is the impression in the video of the character number 7, hence, within the function braces you can declare a variable as *char* b = 7, and then order print it (% c).

CHAPTER 3

DECLARATIONS
The types *char, int, float, and others*

Although in some languages we can use variables without having them previously declared, in C, as in Pascal, this is not allowed. All variables must have its type declared before use, either locally, within a module keys, or globally.

The types of data used for declaring variables, functions or types are:

Type	Range	Number of bytes
char	-128 a +127	1
double	1.7E-308 a 1.7E+308	8
float	3.4E-38 a 3.4E+38	4
int	-32768 a +32767	2
long	-2147843648 a +2147483647	4
long double	1.7E-308 a 1.7E+308	8
short	-32768 a +32767	2
unsigned char	0 a +255	1
unsigned int	0 a +65535	2
unsigned long	0 a +4294967295	4
unsigned short	0 a +65535	2
far	pointer	4
huge	Pointer	4
near	Pointer	2
void	-	-

The expression 3.4E-38 means 3.4x10-38, which is the famous scientific notation of numbers. A number such as 183000 can be written as 1.83E+05, because the dot (floating point) has jumped five orders since the last zero until the first digit non-zero, in the case, the number 1.

In addition to the types seen above, C language also contains modifiers of classes, or types of data, some very simple, others more complicated. Here they are:

> *enum* name {int1, ..., intn}
> *auto* tipo var;
> *register char* var, or *register int* var;
> *extern* type var;
> *static* type var;
> *typedef* type name;
> *const* type name;
> *volatile* type name;
> *struct* name {type v1; type v2; ...; type vn;} vname;
> *union* {type v1; type v2; ...; type vn} vname;

The *enum* type is an ordered set of integers with values 0, 1, 2, ... In *enum* value {a, b, c, d}, we have a = 0, b = 1, c = 2 and d = 3; but in months *enum* {January = 1, Feb, Mar, Apr} we January = 1, Feb = 2, etc.

The *auto* type declares a local variable, and only is valid at the time when the function is called. Being declared within the function in question, it gets already automatic and does not need be explained.

The *register* type causes the variable to be placed in the registers of the processor, which increases the program's speed, but cannot be used with pointers. An extern variable type is global use in the program and must be declared outside of the modules. The *static* variables remain constant value during the program execution. A name declared as *const* cannot have its value changed at any time during the program execution. The *volatile* variable type has the opposite property to the *const*. The *signed* modifier, to *int* and *char* types, has the inverse role of *unsigned*, used to declare unsigned variables.

The *typedef* keyword is used to create a new type into a program. In *typedef long double* Value, the word Value will declare *long double* variables, as in Value x;.

A structure, *struct*, works as *enum*, but it can accommodate not only integer elements, and does not list them sequentially, and additionally creates types. We can have something like: *struct* Body{*char* n[80]; *int* age; *float* height;}; Body girl[20]; girl[5].age = 23;. Here, we reserve 20 variables girl with the Body structure, and the age attributed to the girl number 5 is 23.

The *union* modifier has the same syntax of *struct*, but it stores various types in the same memory location, allowing to use only one at a time. An example is: *union* Conj {*int* i; *float* v; *unsigned char* k;} trio;. In this case, a variable Conj is already declared automatically at the end of the creating of the *union*, which is the variable trio. We could have done this also in the declaration of the variable girl in the structure of the previous paragraph.

Below is a program that exemplifies the use of variable declarations and their relative sizes:

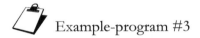 Example-program #3

```
/* Program "Variable.cpp" */
#include <stdio.h>
#define PI 3.1415926
```

int i; *long* k; *short* j; *char* c; *unsigned int* ui;
unsigned long uk; *unsigned short* uj; *unsigned char* uc;
float fl; *double* db; *long double* ld;

```
main()
{
    i=PI*(-1E4); k=-PI*(-1E5); j=i; c=i/30000; ui=-i; uk=-k;
    uj=-j; uc=c; fl=PI; db=fl*(1E-103); ld=db;
    printf("i=%d\t     int\t    %d bytes \n",i,sizeof(i));
    printf("k=%d\t     long\t   ",k);
    printf("%d bytes \n",sizeof(k));
    printf("j=%d\t     short\t   %d bytes \n",j,sizeof(j));
    printf("\nValor          type          size\n\n");
    printf("c=%d\t\t     char\t   %d byte \n",c,sizeof(c));
    printf("ui=%d\t    uns int        %d bytes \n",ui,sizeof(ui));
    printf("uk=%d\t    uns long        ",uk);
    printf("%d bytes \n",sizeof(uk));
    printf("uj=%d\t    uns short     %d bytes \n",uj,sizeof(uj));
    printf("uc=%d\t\t    uns char     %d byte \n",uc,sizeof(uc));
    printf("fl=%f\t    float\t   %d bytes \n",fl,sizeof(fl));
    printf("db=%e     double\t   %d bytes \n",db,sizeof(db));
    printf("ld=%e    long double   ",ld);
    printf("%d bytes \n",sizeof(ld));
}
```

⌒ Modifications to exercise: Try to delete some lines *printf()*, for example the three involving *long* type. For doing this, if you are in the Borland IDE, place the cursor on the line, hold down the Ctrl key and press 'y'. Second amendment: The program uses the *#define* directive, which is to declare a constant with a certain value. This constant is usually written in capital letters. Change the PI identifier for some other constant, with a different value.

Formatting statements for *printf()*

Within the parentheses of *printf()* and other functions we see several preceded symbols '%' or '\', which are, respectively, the replacement character and the escape sequence. Following is a table for these codes:

Code	Meaning	Code	Meaning
%c	character	\f	form feed
%d	integer	\n	line feed
%e	scientific notation	\r	carriage return
%f	floating point	\t	horizontal tab
%g	%e or %f, the shorter	\v	vertical tab
%o	octal unsigned	\\	backslash
%s	String	\?	question
%u	decimal unsigned	\'	apostrophe
%x	hexadecimal unsigned	\"	quotation marks
%%	percent symbol	\nnn	octal number
\a	beep	\xnn	xnn hexadecimal
\b	backspace	'\0'	null terminator

Exercises

1) Write a program that assigns a word or short phrase to a string variable and print; then assign values to two integer variables, not zero, put in a "real" variable ('floating point') the division of the former by the latter (p/n) and print this result (as %f).

2) Write a program that assigns to a numeric variable an integer less than 255, for example 80, and print it on the screen in succession as character (%c), integer (%d), octal (%o) and hexadecimal (%x). If they come in a same print instruction, the variables, after the quotation marks closing, must be separated by commas. If it is k, we have: k, k, k, k.

CHAPTER 4

CONDITIONAL EXECUTION
The *if-else* statement

When Ada Byron, Countess of Lovelace, at the nineteenth century, invented computer programming, to be used in the unfinished Analytical Engine of his friend and mathematical instructor Charles Babbage, she created even in that period what would be the soul of programming, which is running on cycles which require a stopping condition, which, in turn, leads to the need of the conditional execution today mostly used in the form of an *if* statement, introduced by Grace Murray hopper a century later. With the use of cycles and recursion, Ada realized that the Analytical Engine, unlike the previous Difference Engine, could solve any problem with coded instructions previously granted, which was made by punched cards, created by Joseph Marie Jacquard in 1805, which we used until 1975, or a little More than that. She wrote that a problem that required 330 cards could be solved with only three, if she used the cycles. Concerning to the scope of the machine, she said in 1843 that if properly we transformed notes and durations in abstract algebraic codes, the machine would be able to "compose elaborate and scientific pieces of music of any degree of complexity or extent", as Stephen Wolfram.

In the most of the high-level languages, the appearance of a simple *if* statement is as follows:

if (condition)

    statement 1

[*else*

    statement 2].

In Pascal we have a line with the following statement: *if* x>0 *then write* ('Positive!') *else* n: = x;. In C language there is no word *then* and the condition lies within parentheses. An example is the following mini-program:

```
main( ){ int n; char c; puts("\nN/Y?"); c=getchar();
    if(c=='S'){printf("\n True!");n=1;} else n=0; printf("\nn=%d",n);}
```

To run the mini-program is necessary to start with the *#include* *<stdio.h>*. Unless it come more explicit some other file, all mini-programs of this book will only use the *stdio.h* header file.

In C, as mentioned before, the equality in the attributing is "=", while in the comparing, as in the case of the *if*, it is "= =". In the above example, the statement 1 needed braces, because it is composed of more than one instruction; unlikely, the statement 2, after *else*, dispenses braces by containing only one statement in it. Many error messages about the *if* statement refers to the use of "=" instead of "= =". For the simple equality, "=", C allows multiple assignment, unlike older languages. We can write, for example, x = y = z = 10;.

The *switch-case* statement

The *if* statement can be used in nestled form, an *if* inside another, but in the case of multiple options for decision-making is preferable to use the *case* statements, which are started in C with the *switch* keyword. To prevent that the execution includes the following options to valid option, we finished the *case* statement with a *break* statement, a word that can also be used in other situations, not only in the *switch-case* statements, and has as its opposite the *continue* statement.

The program below illustrates the use of *if* and *switch* statements:

Example-program #4

```
/* Program "Multiple.cpp" */
#include <stdio.h>
#include <stdlib.h>

char s[80];
 int k;
 long n;
 main( )
 {printf("\nDividing by 3. Type integer greater than zero:\n");
   gets(s); n=atol(s); k=n%3;
   if (k>=0)
   { switch(k)
     { case 0:
        printf("%d is multiple of 3.",n);break;
       case 1: printf("Remainder 1."); break;
       case 2: printf("Remainder 2."); break;
       default:
        printf("It seems an error has occurred.");
     }
   }
   else printf("Negative valor."); return 0;
 }
```

Modifications to exercise: A first change that the program entails is the changing of the divider on the operator congruence modulo *n*. Instead of testing the divisibility by 3, why one does not it by 4? To do this, replace k = n%3 for k = n%4 and add a line before the *default* line with the words: *case* 3: *printf*("Remainder 3."); *break*;. A second possible change is concerning to the notation and it will show that the computer is not at all sympathetic. If instead of the remains 0, 1 and 2, the content of *k* are alphanumeric, for example, the vowels 'a', 'e' and 'i', so in *case* lines each content is written in single quotes, as spelled in the back. Try this with the numbers 0, 1 and 2 to see what happens.

Note that the number *n* is read from the keyboard as a string *m*, being transformed after into a digital content by the *atol*() function, which changes the argument alphanumeric (ASCII) for the integer type *long*. The functions *atoi*() and *atof*() turn on alphanumeric *int* and *float* respectively. As there is not among the keywords of C instructions for input and output of data, we have to make use of library functions.

After compile, link-edit and run the program through the Run window, open the Window tab and press *Output*. In the IDE Borland you can alternatively type User Screen. This is similar to, without opening the Window tab, press Alt + F5. To return, press any key. If you are in the Output, press Close in the Window tab.

If you are using Gnu, things are also easy. If the source program, written in Notepad or another text editor, was saved as Multiple.c, in the C:\mingw\programs, then open the command prompt and being in the mingw\bin folder, just write: *gcc \mingw\programs\Multiple.c –o Multiple* and the compiler generates the Multiple.exe program. Now just write in the screen thje word Multiple, and hit Enter.

Using the command line in Borland C++ 3.0 is even simpler. Being in the \Borland\bin or \TurboC\bin, according to your folder, simply type *tcc \mingw\programs\Multiple.c* for the program to generate the executable in the Bin folder TurboC. Note that, if instead of tcc we write tc, we are led to the IDE.

The conditional operator

In addition to the *if-else* and *switch-case* statements, C has as its specialty the operator "?", to address the processing conditions. Its use has the syntax

<Condition> <expr1>: <expr2>

and determines that the transaction value will be <expr1> if <condition> is true and <expr2> if it is false. In the statement

x = (k>0) 50: 40

if k>0, the value of x is 50, otherwise we have x = 40. It is equivalent to state *if* (k>0) x = 50; *else* x = 40; but the result produces a more compact writing.

Exercises

1) Make a program that take a number entered on the keyboard and decide (with *if-else*) if it is equal to or greater than (>=) 100 or if it is lesser, printing this information. (Make n = *atoi*(s), to transform the string in number, *atoi*() is in *stdlib.h*.)

2) Create a program that decides if a number entered on the keyboard is even or odd. In the first case, print the message "It is even number." Otherwise, print: "It is odd number." A way to test arithmetically whether a number is pair is to do: *int* x = k/2; *if* (x/2 == k) ...;. Do before x = *atof*(s)., with *s* being the string that receives the number from the keyboard.

CHAPTER 5

FLOW CONTROL - The *while* and *for* statements

The computer programming would not be very useful if, even with the condition assessment instructions, the execution could not go back and resume formulas already used to assign them new values a number of times. Imagine the embarrassment that it would be the simple printing of numbers from zero up to a thousand. With commands that allow the use of iterated variables, this is no problem.

The *while* loop

Printing the numbers from zero to a thousand is easier than taking candy from a baby:

```
main( ){int k=0; while(k<=1000){printf("%d ",k);k+=2;}}
```

Stating how integer the variable k; and initializing it to zero, the mini-program above tells the processor that while k is lesser than or equal to a thousand it should print k, then add 2 to the printed value and return to the word *while*. The instruction "k + = 2;" uses the "+=" symbol, exclusive of C, and it would be written in Pascal as "k: = k+2," meaning that the value of k should be assigned the old variable value plus 2. If you want to run example above, be sure to add at the beginning the line *#include <stdio.h>*.

The *do-while* loop

Another version of the *while* statement is given with the *do-while* couple, the use of which in some cases is more convenient. The difference is that the evaluation condition is made at the end of the loop. The same mini-program above would look like this:

```
main( )
     {int k=0; do{printf("%d ",k);k+=2;} while(k<=1000);}
```

Note that in C it doe not matter if we write "*int* k; k = 0;" or "*int* k = 0;".

The *for* statement

Using the *for* statement in C offers more powerful capabilities than what happens with the same statement in other languages. As C has a very short form of this command, the reader should see an example in Pascal, which uses it in a very similar way to the other languages. To make a loop to rotate from 1 to 100 in Pascal, we have for example: *for* i: = 1 *to* 100 *do begin* y = *ln*(i); *end*;.

In C language, the example is written as:

```
main( ) {int i; float y; for(i=1;i<=100;i++) {y=log(i);printf("\n%f",y);}}
```

The logarithm above is the natural one, because, in C, decimal logarithm is *log*10(). The use of these functions requires writing *#include <math.h>* at the beginning of the program. To run the mini-program above use, therefore, the *stdio.h* and *math.h* header-files.

Inside the parentheses of the *for* we have three statements (initialization; condition; increment). The expression i++ causes the variable i is increased by 1 per spin loop.

There is a slight difference in the order of allocation between using i++ and ++i. In the first case, the variable *i* is incremented and then used; in the second case, it is incremented and used later with the new value already increased of 1.

The *for* statement in C allows the use of more than one variable at a time. The information inside the parentheses is separated by commas for each element where this is necessary. Example:

```
main( ) {int k,m,t,x; t=100; for(k=0,m=t; k<m; ++k,m--) {x=k*m;
    printf("\n%d",x);}}
```

Unlike what happens in Pascal, in C language the *for* statement allows variables as limiters, as in this case, which calculates the number of diagonals of the polygon. Example:

```
main( ) {int d,n,m=50; for(n=m;n>2;n--) {d=n*(n-3)/2;
    printf("\t n=%d -> d=%d",n,d);}}
```

Unconditional jump

An old programming feature that is not used in the construction of structured programs is the *goto* statement. Writing in any height of the program the *goto* statement LABEL; does the control of the execution to be diverted unconditionally to the line initiated by the label followed by a colon, LABEL:. Obviously, the *goto* statement also works for conditional branches, but it is not the most appropriate way to do this. You can have a small program like this below, that, to use an old feature, takes to spell the incrementing j as "j = j + 1;" instead of "j++;":

```
main( ) {int j=0;
    RETAKE: if(j<11) {printf("\n%d",j); j=j+1; goto RETAKE;}}
```

After using an *if* statement, avoid writing in the same line a second instruction, because it can happen to the processor to ignore it. It is the case of the above example, whereas the scope of the *if* goes up to the brace closing.

The program below illustrates the use of *while* and *for*. It draws on screen bar of asterisks in the size determined by the number entered, forming, in fact, a bar graph. If this number is negative, the *while* loop evaluates the condition as false, and the program finishes. It is the stop condition.

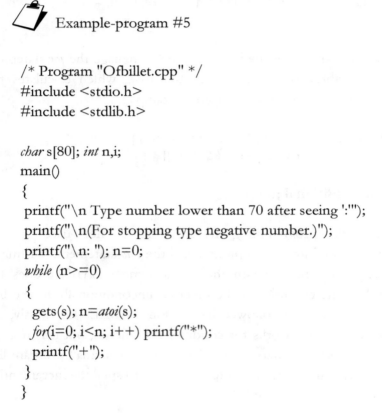 Example-program #5

```
/* Program "Ofbillet.cpp" */
#include <stdio.h>
#include <stdlib.h>

char s[80]; int n,i;
main()
{
printf("\n Type number lower than 70 after seeing ':'");
printf("\n(For stopping type negative number.)");
printf("\n: "); n=0;
while (n>=0)
  {
  gets(s); n=atoi(s);
  for(i=0; i<n; i++) printf("*");
  printf("+");
  }
}
```

Modifications to exercise: A simple change that can be done is to replace the symbol "*" for any other, avoiding "\" and "%", which have special meanings in the format. A second change is the inclusion of a line *for* immediately before the one that is already in the program. To open the space, push the cursor to the left end of the existing line *for* and press Ctrl+N. In this loop one prints a number of spaces, eight for example, to precede the sequence of asterisks in each row. The variable of the new *for* can be the same i (i=0; i<8; i++).

Exercises

1) Write a program that prints the message " Hi!" for a given number of times, within a *while* loop. You can use a counter *i* by making i = i + 1 within the loop, printing the message on each pass until a given limit before the condition, for example, *while* (i <100).

2) Develop a program that prints on the screen one line after another, using dash ("_"), until you touch any key previously specified in the message, for example 's' from 'stop'. In the condition of the *while* loop, which prints the line, you should see a variable character, to be completed by the content of the pressed key, as in (c = *getchar*(), before making c! = 's', on the condition). It is appropriate that the statement to print the dash is within a *for* in this case, before c = *getchar*() ;. It will be a loop inside another one.

CHAPTER 6

ARRAYS - The symbol "[]"

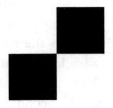

Unlike Pascal, which requires the declaration of array as a variable of type 'array', the C language sees the matrix just as variable of another type, e. g. *char*, and what does it to distinguish a string variable using a simple 'character' of one that stores a series of characters is the presence of brackets in the type declaration.

The declaration *char* k; tells the compiler that in the variable *k* is stored a character. Already the *char* k[30]; statement warns that the variable *k* stores a string of up to 29 characters, always reserving the last position, in case the thirtieth, of number 30, to the null character. The statement k[30] establishes, therefore, a one-dimensional array of 30 positions, going from zero to 29.

Often we name vector to a matrix when it is one-dimensional, so that the term matrix more appropriately will refer to the cases with dimension two, three or more. An array named joan - which reserves 20 positions for the first dimension and 35 for the second - is declared so:

char joan[20][35];

Obviously, we can declare arrays that store values of other different types of *char*. Examples:

int m[25][15][40];
long v[12];
float a[50][20];

A matrix acts as an indexed variable, wherein each index would represent the position of the value. If we declare the array *int* a[4], with values 8, 7, 21 and 5, in this order, the meaning is: $a_0 = 8$, $a_1 = 7$, $a_2 = 21$ and $a_3 = 5$. As in computer programming indexes are not written explicitly, the idea of the indexed variable is held in the matrix.

A very usual exercise in books teaching matrices in the secondary course is one of constructing a matrix whose formula is based on operations with its own contents, for example, matrix A_{2x3} with $a_{ij} = i^2 - j$, aij being any element of this set, *i* indicating the row number and *j* the column number. The following example-program creates and prints a 10x12 matrix built with the formula $a_{ij} = j*(2*i-j)$.

 Example-program #6

```
/* Program "Array.cpp" */
#include <stdio.h>
int i, j, a[10][12];
main( )
{ for (i=1; i<=10; i++)
  for (j=1; j<=12; j++) a[i][j]=j*(2*i-j);
  printf("\n\n\t\t Example of two-dimensional array\n\n");
  for (i=1; i<=10; i++)
  { printf("\n\t ");
    for (j=1; j<=12; j++) printf("%4d ", a[i][j]);
  }
  printf("\n");
}
```

$\mathcal{G\!\!\!\!\!\smile}$ Modifications to exercise: The first proposed amendment is to change the limits in the declaration, for example, 15 and 11, instead of 10 and 12. In this case, be sure to change the limits also within each *for* statement. Second amendment: change the formula: j*(2*i-j) to any other. There exists a multitude of possibilities, for example, 3*i, 2*j, j-i, j*(2*j-i), ... Third change: declare the array as the *float* a[10] [12];, a line below *int* i, j;, erasing the a[10][12] of this line. The formatting "%4d" can be changed then to "%5.1f", and the ten areas of the *printf()* must be reduced to eight.

In the penultimate *printf()* of the program we see the formatting "%4d". It tells the program to print the numbers with four fields. For example, the number 23 is __23.

Initialization of arrays

Arrays can be initialized at the time of the statement identifier, as with the other types. They should, however, be global variables. It is enough that we equalize the array to a sequence of values given between braces. Examples:

> *int* week[7]={1,2,3,4,5,6,7};
> *char* c[5]={'a','l','i','c','e'};
> *int* m[3][2]={{7,5},{3,9},{20,6}};
> *int* week[]={1,2,3,4,5,6,7};

Exercises

1) Write a program that creates a one-dimensional array, a[i], of 15 terms, filled with values given by a formula using the variable *i*, and print it on one line.

2) Make a program that reads and store in a two-dimensional array the first name of people who give hours on a department, with

the lines being week of the lunar month, 1 to 4, and the columns being the numbers of workdays of the week: 2, 3, 4, 5 and 6. These people's names must be entered on the keyboard after a message that asks for them. Remember that two-dimensional array is, after all, a double entry table (Lewis Carroll diagram). To print the table in the video, the column headers can come up with abbreviations of days (Mon, Tue, Wed, Thu, Fri), instead of numbers. Note that, if the array is *m*, calls to it are m[i][j], but the statement at the beginning is something like *char* m[5][7][20];, 20 being the maximum number of characters more one of the names of people, since it is a strings array.

CHAPTER 7

ADDRESS POINTERS - The symbol "&"

Whenever a variable is declared, it is immediately allocated in a particular memory address, which can be accessed by a numerical reference, as occurs with residences, identified by its number in the street. A variable has therefore two kinds of value: the left value, which is its address, and the right value, which is its content. If we do not give any warning to the processor, the value to be manipulated by the programmer in the variable is that of its content, not the address. To deal with the left value of the variable we must declare it as 'pointer', an indicator or pointer of an address.

The only difference between a variable of type pointer and any other variable is that it must be preceded by an asterisk, '*', at the time of declaration, as in *int* a, b, *pa;. For a pointer indicating the address of the variable, we precede this one of the address symbol, '&', like, for example, in:

pa = &a;

We can have a mini-program with the following features:

```
main( ) {int a,b,*pa; a=15; pa=&a; b=*pa; printf("\nb=%d",b);}
```

What we have here is the variable *a* to receive the value 15, with pa pointing to the address and then the variable *b* receiving the content, the number 15, through the pointer pa.

The idea of dynamic allocation

The dynamic programming, or dynamic memory allocation, is a very important resource in the computation and is only possible with the use of pointers through the functions *malloc()*, *calloc()*, *realloc()* and *free()*. In this system, memory addresses go being occupied or dynamically released during the processing phase, to the extent possible. In ordinary programming, non-dynamic, variable declarations, especially of matrix, reserve enough space in memory, regardless of being used effectively, they can not be reallocated for other purposes while the program is running.

Operations with pointers

We cannot multiply or divide pointer variables. But there is a large number of operations that can be made with them. We have: (a) assigning value zero; (b) increment or decrement; (c) addition or subtraction of integers; (d) equality tests (=), intersection (&&) and union (| |); (e) conversion between types of pointers; (f) operations and comparisons with arrays of elements.

Types of pointers

In addition to simple variables pointers, we also have pointers to arrays, structures, pointers, pointers to functions and pointers to pointers.

An array declared as a pointer can work like any other array. That's what happens in this example:

```
main( ) {int i; char *m[]={"o","l","g","a"};
    for(i=0;i<4;i++) printf("\n%s\n ",m[i]);}
```

Note that the print format is "% s", string, not "% c", character. The significance of this is that the pointer *m points to an array of strings, which is how the compiler deals with the letters 'o', 'l', 'g' and 'a'. We can therefore declare a pointer array as

char *vector[] = {"not", "fear", "this."};.

It is possible to execute, so, the following example:

```
main( ){char *ma[]={"Lily","Eve","Mary"};
    int i,t=sizeof(ma)/sizeof(char*);  for(i=0;i<t;i++)puts(ma[i]);}
```

A character pointer, like any other, can allocate dynamic memory in a program. We have the following mini-program:

```
main( )
    {char s,*ps; ps=(char*)malloc(2); s='c'; ps=&s; puts(ps);}
```

The *puts()* function is in the library *stdio.h* e the *malloc()* function, with its associated *calloc()*, *realloc()* and *free()*, are in *stdlib.h*. We do not need limit ourselves to what has been presented above. If we start with three directives, *#include <stdio.h>*, *#include <stdlib.h>* and *#include <string.h>*, we can run the following line-program, which uses string pointer, this time allocating and freeing dynamic memory:

```
main( ) {char *ps; ps=(char*)malloc(256);
    ps="PalmyraCity"; puts(ps); free(ps);}
```

A pointer structure requires a little more work. We can write a program like:

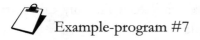 Example-program #7

```
/* Program "Mystruct.cpp" */
#include <stdio.h>
#include <stdlib.h>
```

```
main( )
{
  typedef struct proced {
          char *name[3]; char *loc[3];} Orig;
  Orig *pwho;
  int i;
  pwho=(Orig*)malloc(sizeof(Orig));
  (*pwho).name[1]="Rachel";
            (*pquem).loc[1]="Parati";
  (*pwho).name[2]="Miriam";
            (*pwho).loc[2]="Recife";
    for(i=1;i<3;i++)
    printf("\n%s - %s\n", (*pwho).name[i],
    (*pwho).loc[i]);
}
```

✍ Modifications to exercise: Firstly, increase the limit of the content of matrices *name* and *loc* in the *proced* structure in order to add other lines of name and location before the *for* loop. You must then also increase the limit of the variable *i*. The second amendment is to eliminate all brackets, with their contents, leaving as data line only the first, with "Rachel" and "Parati". In this case press Enter just before the *printf()* and delete the expression for(i = 1; i<3; i++), which is no longer required, as well as the declaration *int* i;. The third amendment, based on the original program, is adding another element in the *proced* structure. After *name and *loc, add, for example, the position for the unity of the federation, the State. Can be *char* *st;. Enter your information: (*pwho).st[1] = "RJ" ;.

Note that the *typedef* type creates new types for declaration and, used in combination with *struct*, as in the program above then created the new type Orig, with what one might declare the pointer *pwho, just as it would do with *char*, in *char* *pwho;, or *int*, in *int*

*pwho;. (An alternative way of writing '(*pwho).name =' is 'pwho>name =').

Finally, as a last kind of pointer, the pointer of pointer is an expression of the form *int* **pn;, and its utility is higher in case of the use of arrays. A pointer called pmatrix, assigning pmatrix = mat accesses the first element of the array mat, that with index zero, and hence *(pmatrix + 1) accesses the second element, *(pmatrix + 2) accesses the third, and so on.

Input and output - *scanf()*

The main functions for video at data output handling are *putchar()*, for characters, *puts()*, for strings, and *printf()*, for formatted output to any symbolic results, as we have seen.

For data entry by the keyboard, the inverse functions of the three above are *getchar()*, *gets()* and *scanf()*. The latter, reverse of *printf()*, is the formatted input function and was presented only at this point of the text because its arguments must necessarily contain pointers. The general form of *scanf()* is *scanf*(format, var1, var2, ...);.

Here it is an example of how to use the *scanf()* function:

```
main( ){char n[80];int k;puts("Digite nome e idade:\n");
     scanf("%s %d", &n,&k); printf("%s    %d\n",n,k);}
```

Except for the code "%g", all format codes starting with the symbol "%" and used in the *printf()* function can also be used in the *scanf()* function. Are the codes %c, %d, %f, %h, %o, %s, %x and %%.

Exercises

1) Write a program that read with *scanf()* a character typed on the keyboard and print it soon after ten times on the same line, with *printf()* in a *for*.

2) Make a program that reads a number of floating point typed

on the keyboard (read with *scanf()*, using the symbol '&' in the variable), assign to a variable pointer the address of the numeric variable that stores this number and then print such contents, first of the common variable, then of the pointer (with an asterisk in the print instruction). If the numerical variables were declared *v* and *px, the assigning of the address will be made as px = &v;.

CHAPTER 8

LOGICAL OPERATORS
The symbols "&&", "| |" and "|"

Often, in conditional execution of commands, we need to write compound conditions, using the connectives AND and OR and the adverb NOT, which are called Boolean operators, because they have been mathematized by George Boole, in 1848 (*The Mathematical Analysis of Logic*). In C language, as we have seen, these words are represented by the symbols '&&', '| |' and '|', respectively. There are several other connectives as derivatives of these three basic relationships, the main among them being the implication (or 'IMP'), the equivalence (or 'EQV') and the exclusive OR ("XOR").

For two any sentences s and p, we can demonstrate in logic that: (a) sIMPq is equivalent to (NOTs) ORp, (b) sEQVp is equivalent to (sIMPp) AND (pIMPs) and (c) sXORp is equivalent to (sAND NOTp) OR (pAND NOTs).

Let's take in C the sentences k = 1, k! = 1, m%9>0, m%5 = 1 and m%3! = 0. You can write the mini-programs below:

```
i) main( ){int k=1,m=1;
      while(!(k==1)ll(m%9>0)){for(m=1;m<9;m++)printf("\n Hi!");}}
```

```
ii) main( ){int k=1,m=1;
      if((k!=1)ll(m%5==1))&&((m%5!=1)ll(k==1)))puts("Ih!");}
```

iii) main( ){*int* k=1,m=0;
  if(!((k==1)&&(m%3!=0))||((m%3==0)&&(k!=1)))puts(*"Ok!");}

The mini-program i exemplifies the use of implication: and, in the case, !(k = 1) is equal to (k! = 1). The example ii shows the equivalence, while iii shows the use of exclusive OR ("XOR"), so-called symmetric difference.

Much attention in the evaluation of each sentence within a cycle, because, if it is always true, the program enters eternal loop, i. e., it will not stop condition. In such a situation, just by pressing Ctrl + Break you will be safe.

De Morgan's laws

Augustus De Morgan (1806-1871), mathematician friend of Boole, showed that (a) NOT (sORp) is equivalent to NOTs AND NOTp and (b) NOT (sANDp) is equivalent to NOTs OR NOTp. In programming languages, including C, truth-values, TRUE and FALSE, are understood as 1 and 0, respectively. So we can do the first law test this example:

  main( ) {*if*(!(1||0)==(!1&&!0)) puts("\n It's right!");}

With the next, we can make the verification of the second law:

  main( ){*if*(!(1&&0)==(!1||!0)) puts(" This works!");}

Axioms of Aristotle

Formal Logic was invented by Aristotle from three basic axioms, which he called:

A) Contradiction principle (N(Ns) is equivalent to s);
B) Excluded middle principle (s is valid or Ns);
C) Principle of identity (s is equivalent to s).

In the above lines, *s* is any sentence and N means "not", "denial" or "to deny" (principles A and C were already used by other philosophers, then Aristotle has brought the principle B). When John Von Neumann directed the construction of the ENIAC computer in 1945, he introduced the so-called "Von Neumann architecture", assembly of the processor that operates on the axioms of Aristotle. You can check if the current processor maintains that architecture, writing to the first principle:

```
main( ) {if((!!(1<2))==(1<2))puts("\nPrinciple 1 is valid.");}
```

For the second principle, we make:

```
main( ) {if((1<2)||(!(1<2)))puts("\nPrinciple 2 is valid.");}
```

For the principle of identity, the test is:

```
main( ) {if((1<2)==(1<2))puts("\nPrinciple 3 is valid.");}
```

Once the comparison of the *if* is made between the truth values of sentences, the comparative equality, '= =', also has the meaning of "is equivalent to", i. e., compares equivalence. The truth value of '1<2' is 1 and the one of '1>2' is 0. Thus, to write a true sentence, type '1', as was done in the above exemplification of Morgan's laws.

The following program illustrates the use of Boolean operator '&&':

 Example-program #8

```
/* Program "PascalTr.cpp" */
#include <stdio.h>
#include <stdlib.h>

int m[20][20]; char p[80];
int i,j,k,n;
main( )
{ printf("\n Type integer lower than 20:\n");
   gets(p); n=atoi(p);
   if (n>0 && n<16)
   { printf("\n\n   Pascal Triangle: ");
      m[1][1]=1; m[2][1]=1; m[2][2]=1; k=4;
      printf("\n\n\n   1\n   1   1");
      for(i=3;i<=n+1;i++) for(j=1;j<=n+1;j++){
         m[i][j]=m[i-1][j-1]+m[i-1][j];}
      for(i=3;i<=n+1;i++)
         { j=2;printf("\n   1");while(j<k && k<=n+2)
            { printf("%4d",m[i][j]); j++;
            } k++;
         }
      printf("\n\n");
   }
   else if (n<=0) printf("Negative number.");
         else if (n>15)
         printf("n>15:It does not fit in the screen.");
}
```

Modifications to exercise: Transform the final two lines, beginning with *else*, in a single line, using the symbol "||", of the connective OR. To do this, type in the *if* condition, within the

49

parentheses, the expression 'n<2 or n>15', translating it to C; then print the message "The number must be positive and lesser than 16", using the *printf()* function. Second amendment: Before closing the last brace, which is the closing of the *main()* function, write a statement to print a dotted line on the screen, to Pascal's triangle end. Start it taking the cursor to the beginning of the line of the last brace and pressing Ctrl + N. This line to be printed on the screen can be drawn with the symbol of 'underscore' ("_"), which should be part of an argument *puts()* or a *printf()* inside a *for* loop. The variable may be i, j, k, or any other resembling integer. Third amendment: Perhaps you have not noticed, but the *if* that was created in the first amendment above is optional, or more than that, unnecessary. Instead of *else if(...) printf(...);*, you can just write *else printf()*.

Note that the construction of Pascal's triangle in the program used to Stifel's Relation: the sum of two adjacent numbers on the line results in the low number, such as 4   6

10.

Bitwise operators

Three logical operators are used in bitwise operations. They are the connectives '&' (bitwise AND), '|' (bitwise OR) and '^' (bitwise XOR). The other bitwise operators are '<<' (scroll to the left, 'left shift'), '>>' (scroll to the right, 'right shift') and '~' (complementary of one, which is unary operator). Any of these operators can only be used with integers or characters.

Taking a = 0x03A1 and b = 0x12B0, we have: a&b = 0x02a0, a|b = 0x13B1 and a^b = 0x1111. What happens is that the operator '&' turns into zeros the bits that in both variables are not equal to 1 and maintains as 1 those that are 1 in equivalent positions of the two numbers. Applied to binary numbers 1001 and 1110, it would produce the number 1000. We have such a mini-program:

```
main( ) {int m,k,p; m=0x101A; k=0x1001; p=m&k; printf("\n%x",p);}
```

The operator "|", the bitwise OR, transforms in 1 the bit that is 1 in one of the numbers or in both. For example, under this operator, the binary numbers 1010 and 1100 produce the number 1110, also binary.

You can try something like:

```
main( ) {int m,k,h; m=0x1094; k=0x0F0C; h=m|k; printf("\n%x",h);}
```

The difference between the OR and XOR operators is as it follows: in the aORb expression is valid what is valid for *a* and also for *b*, simply; but in the aXORb is valid what is valid in *a* but not in *b* or what is valid in *b* but not in *a*. In Set Theory this corresponds, for two sets A and B, to what is called symmetric difference between A and B; which is given by (A-B) È(B-A). In C language we can see the XOR operator, denoted by '^', exemplified in:

```
main( ) {int m,k,n; m=0x04A2; k=0x1D0A; n=m^k; printf("\n%x",n);}
```

The left shift operator ('<<') shifts to the left in the given variable the number of positions specified on the right. For example, n=p<<4 makes *n* to contain the bits of *p*, but with four places out of phase to the left, which multiplies the number by 24. It is a very fast way to multiply a hexadecimal number by powers of 16. An example might be:

```
main( ) {int m,k; m=0x001A; k=m<<8; printf("\n%x",k);}
```

The right shift operator ('>>') works similarly as above, but it moves bits to the right, obviously. An example of using this operator is:

```
main( ) {int m,j; m=0xF2B0; j=m>>4; printf("\n%x",j);}
```

For the inversion of all bits of a variable you can use the operator complementary of 1 ('~'). With this unary operator, all bits of value 1 become zero and all bits that are zero get with value 1. Thus, the binary number 1001 would be 0110. An example of the use of this operator is:

main( ) {*int* m,i; m=0x000A; i=~m; printf("\n%x",i);}

Note that a digit of a hexadecimal number (0xnnnn) is four digits of a binary number, because the hexadecimal digit of higher value, F, which has value 15, is written as 1111 in binary base.

As the reader knows, hexadecimal digits are 0, 1, 2, 3, 4, 5, 6, 7, 8, 9, A, B, C, D, E and F. The advantage of using hexadecimal is that its conversion to the binary code processor is made of a far more quickly way than what occurs with a number given in the base ten.

The truth table

From the propositional calculus, or as Boolean wanted, the algebra of logic, we get the tables with the truth values of sentences compositions. For sentences *s* and *p* and using T and F to "True" and "False", we have:

s p	sANDp	s p	sORp	s	NOTs
T T	T	T T	T	T	F
T F	F	T F	T	F	T
F T	F	F T	T		
F F	F	F F	F		

s p	sXORp	s p	sIMPp	s p	sEQVp
T T	F	T T	T	T T	T
T F	T	T F	F	T F	F
F T	T	F T	T	F T	F
F F	F	F F	T	F F	T

Peirce's logical gates

Charles Sanders Peirce, in the nineteenth century, was who realized the possibility to reproduce in electrical circuits the results observed in Boolean operators. The operators AND, OR and NOT are as follows:

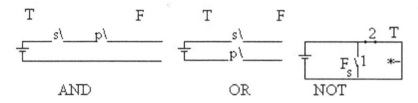

In the AND circuit (in series), the T signal, which is the passage of current, will reach the end node when the s and p doors are closed, i. e., when they are True. In the OR circuit (in parallel), the current T does not reach the end node only when s and p are both in off, or False, as it is the illustration above, all this as the AND and OR tables seen before. In the NOT circuit, when we turn on the switch (1), we cut the link above (2), turning off the light, and vice versa.

The symbols for the three ports in the electronics are:

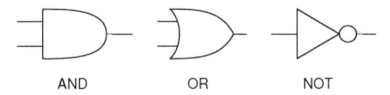

Exercises

1) Using the Aristotelian principle of contradiction, make a program that compares within an *if* the sentence !!(1>0), which is true, with a sentence represented by a single value, 0 or 1, true or false, in a variable *k*, obtained from reading a number from the

keyboard subjected to remainder operation of the division by 2, printing "T", when the result is 1, or "F", when the result is 0. (Make *gets*(a); n = *atol*(a); k = n%2;, without forgetting to declare before the variables).

2) Write a program that reads from the keyboard a number *n* of four non-zero digits and calculates the remainder of the division by nine (n = k%9; is the calculation of nines-off). Then the program must test this number calculated. If it is lesser than 3 or greater than 6, print it with the message "I hate the center.". Otherwise, print it followed by: "Virtue is at the middle (Aristotle)."

CHAPTER 9

LIBRARY FUNCTIONS - Header files

The header files, or libraries, of the ANSI standard library, are as follows:

assert.h	*setjmp.h*
ctype.h	*signal.h*
errno.h	*stdarg.h*
float.h	*stddef.h*
limits.h	*stdio.h*
locale.h	*string.h*
math.h	*time.h*

The smaller of these libraries are *signal.h* - with only two functions, *raise()* and *signal()* -; *setjmp.h* - with the functions *longjmp()* and *setjmp()*, for non-local jumps - and *assert.h* that just have the function *assert()*, to test assertions, i. e., to verify the validity of expressions.

Each company that developed C++ compilers has added over a certain amount of file headers, but the names in this case are not the same from one brand to another. Where there are more differences is the concerning to the screen manipulation functions. For example, the graphic file in the Turbo C++ is *graphics.h*, whereas in the Microsoft C++ is *graph.h*. Rarely there is correspondence between the functions of video of a compiler and another, but in this area, this phenomenon not only occurs with C language. In not dealing with video manipulation, there is a general agreement among several companies, mainly because of unification efforts of the ANSI.

Mathematical functions

As we have seen before, the mathematical functions are stored, mostly, in the file header called *math.h*. The *stdlib.h* header file contains some mathematical functions, such as the non-elementary functions *abs()* and *rand()*, for absolute value and random number, and the function *div()*, which provides the quotient and the remainder of a division.

The *math.h* file defined by ANSI C contains the functions *acos( )*, *asin( )*, *atan( )*, *atan2( )*, *ceil( )*, *cos( )*, *cosh( )*, *exp( )*, *fabs( )*, *floor( )*, *fmod( )*, *frexp( )*, *ldexp( )*, *log( )*, *log10( )*, *modf( )*, *pow( )*, *sin( )*, *sinh( )*, *sqrt( )*, *tan( )* and *tanh( )*.

The functions *acos()*, *asin()* and *atan()* provide the arc cosine, arc sine and arc tangent. The function *atan2()* uses for the arc tangent two arguments x and y, the two cathetus; *cosh()* is the hyperbolic cosine, whereas *exp()* and *log()* are the exponential and logarithm functions in the base e (natural base $e = 2.718$ ..., the decimal logarithm is *log10()*); *fabs()* gives the absolute (non-negative) value, *modf()* provides the rest of the division between two values, *floor()* and *ceil()* respectively provide the smallest and largest integer contained in the argument (*floor()* in many other languages is *int()*), *pow()* calculates the power, with two arguments, *frexp()* provides a mantissa, from .5 to 1, whereas *ldexp()* provides the result of $x*2^k$, for arguments x and k.

Using *stdio.h* and *math.h* you may experience the following example:

```
main( ) {float x,y,w,t; x=4.81; y=cos(2*log(x+1));
        w=floor(y); t=pow(4,w); printf("\n%f %f %f",y,w,t);}
```

Alphanumeric functions

The alphanumeric functions, or string functions, are contained, mostly, in the header files *ctype.h* and *string.h*.

In the ANSI standard the functions of the *ctype.h* file are: *isalnum()*, *isalpha()*, *iscntrl()*, *isdigit()*, *isgraph()*, *islower()*, *isprint()*, *ispunct()*, *isspace()*, *isupper()*, *isxdigit()*, *tolower()* and *toupper()*. The latter converts an uppercase character ('upper'), whereas *tolower()* converts a lowercase character ('lower'). The other functions check whether the character is of a particular type. So *isalnum()* checks whether the character is alphanumeric, *isalpha()* checks if it is letter of the alphabet, *iscntrl()* checks if it is control character, and so on.

The standard *string.h* header file contains the functions that follow: *memchar()*, *memcmp()*, *memcpy()*, *memmove()*, *memset()*, *strcat()*, *strchr()*, *strcmp()*, *strcoll()*, *strcpy()*, *strerror()*, *strlen()*, *strncat()*, *strncmp()*, *strncpy()*, *strpbrk()*, *strrchr()*, *strspn()*, *strstr()*, *strtok()* and *strxfrm()*. Let's look at some cases. In the expression *memchar(const *s, int c, size_t m)*; the function searches for the character *c* among the first *n* characters of the content pointed to by **s* variable. The statement *char *strcat(char s, const char p)*; concatenate the string *p* at the end of the string *s*. The *strcmp()* function compares two alphanumeric arguments, *strcpy()* copies the string of the first argument in the second, *strncpy()* does the same thing for the first *n* characters and *strlen()* provides the size of a string. The *strcoll()* and *strxfrm()* functions compare strings of different languages. They are not in Turbo C or in Microsoft C.

The example-program below illustrates the use of some alphanumeric functions.

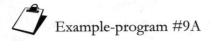 Example-program #9A

```
/* Programa "Alphanum.cpp" */
#include <stdio.h>
#include <string.h>
#define TOTAL 80
void Invert(char s[])
{  int i, k=strlen(s);
   printf("\n");
   for(i=k-1; i>=0; --i) putchar(s[i]);
}
void Space(char s[])
{  int i,k=strlen(s);
   printf("\n");
   for(i=0;i<k;i++){putchar(s[i]); putchar(' ');}
}
main()
{  char s[TOTAL]; char m[TOTAL];
   char p[]="Bed"; char q[]="time";
   printf("\n Type a name:\n"); gets(s);
   Invert(s); printf("\n");
   Space(s); printf("\n");
   printf("\n%s",p); printf("\n%s",q);
   strcpy(m,p); strcat(m,q); printf("\n%s\n",m);
}
```

   Modifications to exercise: The first possible change is the exchange of the words "Bed" and "time" for different sizes of words such as "Page" and "ant". The second amendment is a bit more arduous: to create the Combine() function, which performs the roles of Invert() and Space() at the same time. Third change: change the "Type a name:" to "Type two words:" and create a fourth function, called Merge(), which perform the operations of the current last two lines of instructions in the program, these starting with *printf()* and *strcpy()*. Of course, once you have created the function, these lines should be deleted and in its place it should be a call to the function.

Using the header files *stdio.h*, *string.h* and *ctype.h*, the reader, to create the Merge() function suggested above, can be based on the mini-program below, which gives to the vector *ma* the expression "Aca pulco" and launches at the vector *p* the fused word "Acapulco".

```
main( ){char p[80],m[]="Aca pulco"; int i,k,s=strlen(m);
    printf("\n"); for(i=0;i<=s;i++)if(isspace(m[i])) k=i; strncpy(p,m,k);
    for(i=0;i<=s;i++) {p[i+k]=m[i+k+1];}  printf("\n %s",p);}
```

Other alphanumeric functions

In addition to important utility functions such as *abort()*, *atexit()*, *bsearch()*, *calloc()*, *exit()*, *free()*, *malloc()*, *qsort()*, *realloc()*, *system()*, and some functions mathematics (*abs()*, *div()*, *labs()*, *ldiv()*, *rand()* and *srand()*), the *stdlib.h* header file contains several functions that convert strings to other types of objects. The best-known compilers include the following: *atof()*, *atoi()*, *atol()* *strtod()* *strtol()* and *strtoul()*. The *atof()* function transforms into data type *float* a number entered as a string (ASCII). The *atoi()* function converts the same data type as a whole number and *atol()* in a integer of type *long*. The *strtod()*, *strtol()* and *strtoul()* functions turn on alphanumeric in values of type *long* and *unsigned long*, respectively, but in these last two, who have three arguments, the third of them informs the numeration base.

Using *stdio.h*, *stdlib.h* and *time.h*, you can run the following example, which creates two random numbers, first taking as seed (*srand()*) the number entered by the keyboard, after taking a system value by the *time()* function.

```
main( ) { float k,r1,r2;char s[80];puts("Type number:");gets(s);
   k=atol(s);srand(k); r1=rand( ); srand(time(NULL)); r2=rand( );
   printf("\n%f%f",r1,r2);}
```

Time functions

The default *time.h* header file has the nine functions that follow: *asctime()*, *clock()*, *ctime()*, *difftime()*, *gmtime()*, *localtime()*, *mktime()*, *strftime()* and *time()*. This first function, *asctime()*, provides an alphanumeric string (ASCII) containing day, month, hour, minute, second and year; *ctime()* produces the same string, but you can get the time in *time()*; *strftime()* produces a formatted string; *clock()* gives the number of ticks (18.2 per second) since the start of the program; the *gmtime()* function converts the time in the Greenwich mean time and *difftime()* gives the difference between two times. In the example of the item above the *time()* function takes as argument a NULL constant, the system pointer to null argument. Their types are declared as *time_t* or *clock_t*.

The mini-program below illustrates the use of time-functions.

```
main( ){time_t in,fi;float i;double d;in=time(NULL);
   for(i=1;i<5000000;i++){ }fi=time(NULL);d=difftime(fi,in);
   printf("\nTime: %0.1f seconds.",d);}
```

The *strftime()* function has the following syntax: *size_t strftime(char *s, size_t, tam, const char *format, const *pthour tm);*. Printing *s* we have the string with the time information requested in *format. The function value is the number of characters in *s*. The replacement characters are the following :

%a	abbreviated weekday	%p	AM or PM
%A	day of the week	%S	second (0-59)
%b	abbreviated month name	%U	week of the year (0-53)
%B	Month name	%w	day (0-6)
%c	local time and date	%W	week of the year (on Monday)
%d	day (1-31)	%x	date location representation
%H	hour (0-23)	%X	local representation of the hour
%I	hour (1-12)	%y	year (0-99)
%J	day of the year (1-366)	%Y	year (four digits)
%m	month (1-12)	%Z	time zone name
%M	minute (0-59)	%%	percent symbol

Arguments of functions

When a function receives a value to be processed, we use to name it 'argument'. The variables inside a function intended to receive external values are called 'parameters'. In a program, variables declared within the function prototypes are automatic variables, even if you do not use the word *auto*, because they act only when the function is called, without existing out of it.

The argc and argv parameters

Also the *main()* function can take parameters beyond the word *void*. They are the special *argc* ("argument count") and *argv* ("argument vector"), which receive content external to the program.

The terms from the command line, for example, may be transferred to the *main()* program through these arguments, as in the mini-program below:

```
main(int argc, char *argv[]){int i;printf("Number:%d\n",argc);
for(i=0;i<argc;i++)printf("\n%d:  %s\n",i,argv[i]);}
```

If you are using an environment (IDE), the words typed in "argument", of the Run tab, will be the contents of the successive positions of the vector *argv[]*, the next time you run the mini-program. The terms *argc* and *argv* are variable, and can be replaced by other words.

The technique of "swap"

Many are the algebraic techniques used in programming, which sometimes have to resort to resources that we might call para-algebraic, like this of assigning different values to the same variable (x = 1, x = 2, x = 3) within the same problem. Some languages resolve this difference of handling, between algebra and programming, adopting a special symbol, indicating that this equality is only a value assignment, which may be temporary. Therefore, they do x: = 1 x: = 2, etc. In C, the programmer should be concerned only with the difference between the symbol of equality in the assigning, which is "=", and in comparison, which is "= =". When in the program x is worth 2, then it is worth 4, what we have is $x_1 = 2$ and $x_2 = 4$, with the dispensation of the written of these indexes, which are implied.

And what happens, in any language, when the programmer assigns a value given to the variable x and needs to change this value by one that was assigned to the variable y? Because if we make y = x, the value previously stored in y disappears, and we will not have how to rescue it to put it in x. This is solved with the techniques named "swap". The most common is to introduce a third variable, w, for example. We attribute the value of x to w, and then deposited in x the value of y. Then we attach to y the value that was stored in w, which was the old value of x.

A classic use of this swap technique is necessary for the program to calculate the Highest Common Factor (HCF) of two numbers. To compute this value, we divide the largest of them by the smaller, and, if the result, the quotient, is not 1, we return to the division, now of the divider by the remainder. We repeat this step, making the division of the divider by the remainder, until obtaining quotient 1. The last divider then will be the sought HCF.

In the program-example below, establishing a HCF function, the variables m and d, which initially store the data values of n and p, need to exchange values between them, and then use the auxiliary variable k.

 Example-program #9B

```
#include <stdio.h>
 long Hcf(int n, int p)
 {
   int m, d, k, r;
   puts("\nType two integers greatest than zero: ");
   scanf("%d",&n); scanf("%d",&p);
   m=n; d=p;
   if(m<d){k=m; m=d; d=k;}
   r=1;
   while(r>0){r=m%d; m=d; d=r;}
   return m;
 }
 main ()
     {int n, p; printf("\nThe HCF is %d",Hcf(n,p));}
```

Another way to the swap technique is to use a somewhat surprising feature. You assign to x the sum of two variables, x + y. Then you assign to y the difference x-y, which now means the sum minus y, i. e., x + y - y. At this point, y has the value that was in the original x. And as the new x is storing the initial sum, simply deduct the new y, which is the old x, making x = x-y. For example, if we have x = 7 and y = 5, we do x = 7+5, which gives x = 12; then we do y = x-y, that now means 12-5, and then we have y = 7; now, x = x-y, which is 12-7, getting x = 5.

Exercises

1) Create a program that, using as arguments the integers 1-20, print in a table, with a precision of hundredths (%.2f), the square root values, *sqrt()*, of the power of *e*, *exp()*, of the decimal logarithm, *log10()*, of the cosine, *cos()*, and of the the arc-tangent, *atan()*. Note

that to print these functions it is enough to take only one print statement inside a loop. A suggestion for formatting is: "\n \t% 2d% 5.2f% 12.2f% 9.2f% 9.2f% 9.2f", where %2d is for the value of the integer argument (1-20) and the following formats are for the functions in the order given above.

2) A curiosity that needs to be explored in programming is the feature that allows you to decide which is the greater of two values without using a symbol of inequality. This is possible with the use of the absolute value function. Assume that the program has generated two digits, *a* and *b*, through the random function, and you need to know what is the lowest. The mini-program below, which uses *stdlib.h* and *time.h*, obtains the two numbers. The use of "time" is so that the random value depends on the moment when the program is executed, otherwise the value of *rand()* will always be repeated.

```
main() {int a,b; srand(time(NULL)); a=10*rand()/32767;
b=10*rand()/32767; printf("\n%d %d",a,b);}
```

To decide the minimum value, the formula in regular algebra, is $m = (a+b-|a-b|)/2$, which translated to C is: $m = (a+b-abs(a-b))/2$. If we want to get the greatest value, not the lowest, just we exchange for "+" the minus sign that appears before the *abs()* function.

The exercise for the reader is to build this program, which, recalling, manages two digits *a* and *b* through the random function, and then decide which of the two values is the lowest, without using the symbol "<", printing then this result.

CHAPTER 10

PREPROCESSOR DIRECTIVES
The symbol "#"

The preprocessor makes analysis and operations in the source code before the program is passed to the compiler. Among these tasks they are text strings, mergers, conditional compilation execution, directive signaling and including of other files in the source program.

The preprocessor directives should take independent lines in the program and make it possible to the processor to inform on the tasks that precede the compilation. The following are the default directives: *#define, #undef, #include, #if, #ifdef, #else, #elif, #ifndef, #if defined(), #endif, #error, #line* and *#pragma*.

The *#include* directive is the most used and serves to instruct the processor to use in the program the file cited among the symbols '<' and '>'. Examples: *#include <stdlib.h>, #include* "calculus.h" *#include <C:\clipper\mel.h>*. (The symbol '#' is said "cardinal", or, simply, "number".)

Another directive widely used is *#define*, whose role is to define a term for the compiler and, where appropriate, assign an alphanumeric content to this term. Examples: *#define* CITY Paris, #define FACE, #define MAX 50. (Note that there is neither the equal sign nor semi-colon.)

The *#undef* directive has the opposite role to that of *#define*, serving to warn the processor to "undefine" a term. Its use is necessary before making a redefinition of the same word. The *#if* and *#else* directives act as *if* and *else*, but, as *#ifdef*, *#ifndef*, *#endif* and *#elif*, deals with the situation of directives, exempts the use of parameters in the condition and do not accept other commands on the same line. The *#ifdef* and *#ifndef* terms mean, respectively, "if defined" and "if non-defined"; *#elif* comes from "else if".

The expression *#line* precedes an integer, which indicates the number of the next line in the program and, optionally, a program name, in which also meets the aforementioned line. An example is *#line* 12 "Alphanum.cpp".

The *#if defined()* directive has the role of *#ifdef*, but admits composite sentences, using '&&', '||', etc.

Exclusive directives

The *#pragma* options vary between different compilers and its use allows the compiler to include commands that depend on the implementation. In Turbo C compiler directives are *#pragma inline* and *#pragma warn*; in Microsoft C are: *#pragma pack*, *#pragma loop_opt* and *#pragma check_stack*.

Exclusive of Turbo C, the *#error* directive instructs the processor to send a message in case of error in compile time, as in this example:

```
#ifdef MAX
#error Undefined constant.
#endif
```

The program below illustrates the use of some directives of the preprocessor:

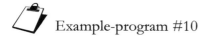 Example-program #10

```
/* Program "Directiv.cpp" */
 #include <stdio.h>
 #include <assert.h>
 #define DEBUG
 #define TOP 200

 main( )
 {
   #if TOP>100
     printf("\n Beginning here.\n");
     #else printf("\n Error!");
   #endif
   assert(TOP<201);
   #ifndef DEBUGR
     printf("\n  Defining DEBUG is missing.");
   #endif
   #ifdef DEBUG
     printf("\n  It is Ok!\n\n");
     #elif defined(TOP)
     printf("\n  Now more than before.\n");
   #endif
   puts("\n   The End!\n");
 }
```

𝒢𝒰 Modifications to exercise: The assertive after the first *#endif, assert*(TOP<201), is true, which causes the program to run normally. Put in place a false sentence to see the error message that the processor will print. Just switch 201 by 200, for example. The second amendment is to change the *#ifdef* by *#ifndef*, doing the number 201 to return in the statement, so that the processing does not stop at that line. The new message to be printed should be the other, formerly skipped. The third change is to replace the former *#ifndef* directive by *#ifdef*, so as to make the true condition and to see printed the message of the *printf()*. If your compiler contains the *#error* directive, replace the *printf()* for it to print the same message.

Exercises

1) Develop a program that defines the constant PI as 3.14159 and also the constant AVOGADRO as 6.02E+23. Then the program prints the cosine value of 2*PI/3 and also the Avogadro's value divided by PI^{23}, i. e. by *pow*(PI, 23). Do not forget to include library *math.h*.

2) Make a program in that is set the constant FEB with the value 28. A message must ask you to type in a given year. Assign to a certain variable the remainder of the division by 4 (if the remainder is zero the year is a leap). Assign to a variable *m* the value of FEB, "undefine" FEB and set it now with the value 29. Test if the year is leap year (i. e., if the rest already calculated is zero) and if so, assign FEB value to the variable *m*. Finally, print the message "Jan: 31 days, Feb: %d days", where %d is replaced in processing by FEB value. Remember that the directives *#define*, *#undef*, etc., should start lines.

CHAPTER 11

HANDLING OF FILES - the *fopen*() function

For Input/Output (or I/O) of data in discs or terminal devices, ports and printers, C language has two forms of handling: the standard input/output, or high level, defined by ANSI, and the system-level input/output, which has been adopted by the UNIX operating system, but has not been included in the ANSI standard.

The streams of I/O are called *stdout* (standard output), *stdin* (standard input, keyboard), *stderr* (error output), *stdaux* (auxiliary device) and *stdprn* (printer).

The high level I/O is also called bufferized I/O, because the flow ('stream') of bytes is stored in a buffer, before being passed to its final destination.

The *stdio.h* header functions for handling files in I/O standard are:

clearerr()	fputc()	getchar()	scanf()
Fclose()	fputs()	gets()	setbuf()
feof()	fread()	perror()	setvbuf()
Ferror()	freopen()	printf()	sprintf()
Fflush()	fscanf()	putc()	sscanf()
fgetc()	fseek()	putchar()	tmpfile()
Fgetpos()	fsetpos()	puts()	tmpnam()
fgets()	ftell()	remove()	ungetc()
fopen()	fwrite()	rename()	vfprintf()
fprintf()	getc()	rewind()	vprintf()
			vsprintf()

In addition to the above functions in the *stdio.h* header file, there are also constants as EOF, NULL and SEEK_SET.

The default function for opening of files is *fopen()*. This function should be used with the syntax FILE **fopen(char* *name, *char* *mode), where *name is the pointer to the file name and *mode tells the computer whether the file is in text mode or in binary mode and if the opening is for reading or writing. In case of error the function returns NULL.

File modes have the following symbols:

Symbol	mode	Symbol	mode
"r"	reading ('read')	"ab"	increase in binary file
"w"	write ('write')	"r+", "w+", "a+"	reading and also
"a"	Increase ('append')		recording
"rb"	binary reading	"r+b", "w+b", "a+b"	idem file binary
"wb"	binary recording		

In some compilers must be written "rb+", "wb+" and "ab+" instead of "r+b", "w+b" and "a+b".

The inverse of *fopen()* function is *fclose()*, which closes any previously opened file. If the file cannot be closed it returns EOF, but if all goes well it returns zero. It must be used with the syntax *fclose*(FILE *stream).

Using headers *stdio.h* and *stdlib.h*, you can try the mini-program below:

```
main( ){FILE *a; a=fopen("file1.xxx", "w"); if(!a) {
    puts("Error!");exit(1);} else printf("Success!");fclose(a);}
```

It is then written an empty file, since nothing has been placed in it. At the command line, you can ask the directory (DIR) and verify that FILE1.XXX is there. The mini-program below can be used to delete it.

```
main( ){int k; k=remove("file1.xxx"); if(k!=0) {
    puts("Error!"); exit(1);} else puts("Success!");}
```

Another mini-program with the same layout and same terms of the above one could have been used to change the name FILE1.XXX file before deleting it, just have just changed the statement k=*remove*("file1.xxx"); for something like this: k=*rename*("file1.xxx", "newname.xxx");.

Writing within files

If *fopen*() and *fclose*() open and close files, which are the appropriate functions so that we can write and read data in them? These functions are *fwrite*() and *fread*(). They should be used as: type *fwrite*(*void* *p, size, n, FILE *stream); and type *fread*(*void* *p, size, n, FILE *stream);, whose arguments represent, in order, the address of the buffer, the size in bytes of this buffer, the number of objects of that size and a FILE pointer.

Before submitting a sample program to illustrate *fwrite*() and *fread*(), let's show the way in which the character manipulation functions must be written. If *c* is a character, these functions are written so: *int getc*(FILE *stream);, *int getchar*(*void*);, *int putc*(*const int* c, FILE *stream);, *int putchar*(*const int* c);, *int ungetc*(*int* c, FILE *stream);, *int fgetc*(FILE *stream); and *int fputc*(*int* c, FILE *stream);.

The *getc*() function, as *fgetc*(), reads a character from any file, whereas *getchar*() reads a character of a input standard device, normally the keyboard. Thus, *getchar*(*void*) is the same as *getc*(*stdin*).

This can be seen in the mini-program below:

```
main( ){char c; printf("\nType character:"); c=getc(stdin);
    printf("Tecla: %4c\n",c); fflush(stdin); printf("Type Enter.");
    while((c=getchar())!='\n'){}}
```

The *fflush*() function records the output content in the file and

71

clears the buffer, releasing it even of possible error messages.

Now, taking *s* as a string, we have the functions *char *gets (char *s);, int puts(const char *s);, char *fgets(char *s, int* n, FILE *stream); and *int fputs(const char *s*, FILE *stream);.

You can try the following:

```
main( ) {char s[256]; puts("Type a phrase: ");
        gets(s); printf("\nThe phrase is: \n,%s",s);}
```

Formatted input

The *scanf()* family, contained in *stdio.h*, has three expressions: *int fscanf*(FILE *stream, *const char* *format);, *int scanf(const char* *format, ...);* and *int sscanf(const char* *s, *const char* *format, ...);. The latter function converts string in binary file. The ellipses here are filled by the sequences of these variables in *const char* *format. Within these functions, the arguments need to point to address.

An example is the mini-program below:

```
main( ){char m[80]; puts("Type phrase: ");fscanf(stdin,  "%s",&m);
        printf("\n Repeating: %s",m); fflush(stdin);}
```

The *scanf()* function assigns to the variable in question the string contents only up to the first space, so the words of the sentence must be connected by some symbol of crossbar. The phrase can be: I_have_learnt_C_language.

Formatted output

The inverse functions of these of the *scanf()* family are the functions *fprintf(), printf()* and *sprintf()*. They should be used with the syntax: *int fprintf*(FILE *stream, *const char* *format, ...);, *int printf(const char* *format, ...);* and *int sprintf(char* *s, *const char* *format, ...);. Note that, except for the call to the file (FILE * stream), the *fprintf()* function is similar to *printf()* and *sprintf()*.

An example is the mini-program below, wherein the matrix *n* comes in *fscanf()* no preceded by '&', because array name is already an address to its first element.

```
main( ){char n[80];int i; printf("\nType name and height in cm:\n");
     fscanf(stdin,"%s%d",n,&i);
     fprintf(stdout, "Name: %s\n Height: %d cm",n,i);}
```

Functions for errors handling

The standard error-handling functions are *clearerr()*, *ferror()* and *perror()* in the *stdio.h* file, besides the *strerror()* function contained in *string.h*. This first function which is used as *void clearerr(FILE *stream);*, cleans and resets to zero the error indicator, in addiction to disconnect the end of file indicator. The second function, which is written in the form *int ferror(FILE *stream);*, check for error in the stream in question, returning zero if there is no error and a non-zero value if an error has been detected. The type of error is identified by the *perror()* function. This has the syntax *void perror(const char *s);* and displays the string *s in the standard error output device *stderr*, and a message to *errno*. The *strerror()* function is used in the form *char *strerror(int errnum);* and returns an error message associated with the error number given by *errnum* argument.

The mini-program below shows the operation of error handling functions:

```
main( ) {FILE *a; a=fopen("Unexist.cpp","r"); if(!a);
     perror("Ugly error!"); clearerr(stdin);}
```

After *perror()* function, and before *clearerr()*, in the line above, we can also add also the *strerr()* function in something like *char *e = strerr(errno); puts(e);*. In this case, they must use the header files *stdlib.h* and *string.h*.

The program below illustrates the use of functions of this chapter. Note that the *fwrite()* function is called twice in a row, one to report on the size of the matrix row and another to move the content. The same occurs with the *fread()* function. Note also that the program could be divided in two separate programs, one for recording and one for reading the same binary file. Within it you can write data lines, which can be, for example, five names of friends with their phones.

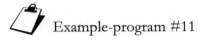 Example-program #11

```
/* Program "Files.cpp" */
#include <stdio.h>
main()
{
  FILE *f; int i,k,total=80; char m[20][80];
  printf("\nType five names:\n");
  f=fopen("arq.bin","w+b");  /* Module saving */
  for(i=0;i<5;i++) {
    fgets(m[i],total,stdin);
    k=fwrite(&total,sizeof(total),1,f);
        k=fwrite(m[i],sizeof(int),total,f);
    if(!k) perror("Error saving!");}
  fclose(f);
  printf("\n");
  f=fopen("arq.bin","r+b");/* Module reading file*/
  for(i=0;i<5;i++) {
    k=fread(&total,sizeof(total),1,f);
        k=fread(m[i],sizeof(int),total,f);
    if(!k) perror("Error reading file.");
    fprintf(stdout,"%s",m[i]);}
  fclose(f);
}
```

Modifications to exercise: The first possible change is for the number of lines in the file. The matrix *m* books 20 positions in the declaration and only five are used (when introducing the fifth row of data, the Enter processes the information). This maximum data lines may be increased to 15, for example, or a number greater than 20 if the limit is increased in the declaration. Second amendment: while changing the *for* command with *while* statements, create a condition with a code ('@', for example) to end the input data lines. The amount *i* of lines will then be somewhat more elastic. The third amendment is to introduce between the two directions k = *fread()* a dynamic memory allocation instruction. In this case, declare a new matrix, *char* *ma, for example, to replace *m*. The declarative will be *char* *ma = *(char*)malloc*(total **sizeof(int)*);. From that point, including the next k = *fread()*, all references to *m* are exchanged for ma and the *stdlib.h* header file should be added at the beginning. The fourth proposed amendment is harder: to transform the two modules in two functions, for example Writeb() and Readb(), with a declarative that allows the user to choose at the start of the main program between to write (record) in the file, with writeb( ), or to read the file, with Readb().

With *stdio.h* and *ctype.h* header files, the mini-program below gives an idea of how to use options for characters typed on the keyboard.

```
main( ){char c;printf("\nType Y or N: ");c=getchar();
    If(toupper(c)=='S') printf("\nIAgree."); else printf("\nI disagree.");}
```

To create a menu with multiple options, not only with 'Yes' or 'Not', you can use the *switch-case* statement instead of *if-else*.

Input and output by keyboard and video

The file-header *conio.h* – it works only on MS-DOS and should not be used therefore in DR-DOS, UNIX, or other operating system – refers to functions relating to I/O of the console (screen/keyboard) and ports.

The following are library functions in *conio.h*:

cgets( )	getche( )	cputs( )	inp( )
Cscanf( )	ungetc( )	putch( )	outp( )
getch( )	cprintf( )	kbhit( )	

To use the above functions, it is not necessary to open or close as files the console or ports. The roles of these functions are similar to the corresponding in *stdio.h* file; as *getche()*, which acts as *getchar()*.

The *kbhit()* function returns a non-zero integer if a key is pressed and returns zero otherwise. It is used to create program-stop device. The functions that relate to ports are *inp()* and *out()*. The Turbo C includes in its header file *conio.h* the screen cleaning function *clrscr()*, name constructed from 'clear screen'. To use it, simply write it anyway, with blank argument: *clrscr();*. The Microsoft C uses for that a very similar function: *_clearscreen()*.

For any type of compiler, you can record a Clear.cpp program, which may become a Clear() function by doing something like:

```
main( ) {int i,j; for(i=0;i<24;i++) {for(j=0;j<10;j++)printf("\t");
    printf("\n");}}
```

The C++ *iostream.h* header file

The Turbo C++ has a powerful file-header I/O functions called *iostream.h*, developed from an earlier name *stream.h*. The *iostream.h* file contains the classes *ios*, *istream_withassign*, *iostream_withassign*, *ostream*, *ostream_withassign* and *streambuf*. In it there are 74 functions, among which we can find *allocate, base, cout, flush, set, hex, peek, put, read, with, write* and *ws*.

Specific features of C++ are useful and bring advantages when we include the use of classes in programming work (class is a type of compound statement, as *struct* and *union*), which is done in 'object-oriented programming' (OOP), for systems with windows. If a class is a type declaration, an object is any element of this class. The teaching of the techniques necessary for such advanced programming philosophy would require another book, dedicated only to the subject.

System-level input and output

The non-bufferized I/O, or low-level, defined by the UNIX, uses the *open()* function instead of *fopen()* to open a file. The inverse function here, to close file, is *close()*, corresponding to the ANSI standard *fclose()*. The flow pointers FILE *flush are here replaced by simple file names and the value that the function returns is an integer called file descriptor, used to identify which file you are working with. The function syntax is *int open*(fname, mode);, which mode is an integer that describes the type of operation, but that, to vary from compiler to compiler, should be replaced by its name, which is a code in capital letters. The options for mode are:

O_APPEND	points the end, for additions
O_CREAT	creates new file
O_RDONLY	opens read only
O_RDWR	opens for reading and writing
O_TRUNC	cleans the file and opens it
O_WRONLY	opens only for writing
O_BINARY	opens in binary mode
O_TEXT	opens in text mode
O_IWRITE	allowed recording
O_IREAD	allowed reading

The header file that contains these options, with the *open()* and *close()* functions, is *fnctl.h*. Other functions contained therein are *read()*, *write()*, *tell()* - which provides the file pointer location - and *lseek()*, which positions the indicator in a certain place.

Much attention is necessary not to mix high level declarative I/O with these non-bufferized I/O, because you cannot use at the same time the two types of handlings. The I/O system, although it is part of most compilers, has been gradually abandoned in favor of standard ANSI usage.

Exercises

1) Write a program that stores the developer's name in a matrix *k*, then compare this content with a name read from the keyboard through the *fscanf()* function, as the item "formatted input" above. If the name is the same, print "Okay!", printing "Nothing doing!" if the name does not match. Finally, clean the buffer, with *fflush()*.

2) Create a program that only read a binary file without saving

it, - for example the file 'file.bin' of the example-program #11 - then transform the alphanumeric content capitalized strings (by the *toupper()* function, *ctype.h*, of the header file, used within a loop with *j*, internal to the loop of *i*, if you are using this variable). Finally, print the result on the screen.

CHAPTER 12

SPECIAL ALGORITHMS

Mathematician Al-Khowarizmi, of Persian Arab origin, who has developed significant algebra techniques, including the first equation-solving methods, has bequeathed us involuntarily two words derived from his name: 'algorithm' and 'algorism'. The first is the fusion of *algorism* with *arithmos*, the Greek word for number. An algorithm is a process built on arithmetic, algebraic or logic base, capable of providing a solution to a problem or perform certain calculations. Examples are the algorithm of the sum, learned in the 1st elementary grade, and the Briot-Ruffini algorithm, in the last year of the high school. If the algorithms did not exist, certainly computer science would not exist also.

Recursion

One of the facilities brought about by the user-defined functions with programming technique is recursion. A recursive function is one that calls itself. In some cases the savings in time and space is huge.

A small example of recursion is used in the program below, which calculates the factorial of a given number. The formula for factorial of n is n! = n(n-1)(n-2) ... 3 × 2 × 1. For a given positive integer value, the factorial is therefore the multiplication of the sequence of numbers from #1 to it. In the program, the successive decrements of n and the products are obtained recursively.

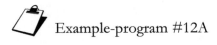 Example-program #12A

```
/* Program "Factori.cpp" */
#include <stdio.h>
#include <stdlib.h>

float Fatori(int n) {
        if (n==0) return 1;
        else return n*Factori(n-1);}
main()
{
   int i; float k; char s[20];
   printf("\nType a positive number: ");
   gets(s); i=atoi(s);
   k=Factori(i); printf("\n n!=%18.0f",k);
}
```

Modifications to exercise: The first change is on the type. The *float* declaration can be changed to *int*, in the function and in the variable *k*. Which are the advantages and disadvantages? The reader knows that with numbers declared as integers the program processing is done much faster. The problem is that only it is possible to calculate up to 7!, for 8! already result in a value greater than 40,000, outside the signalized integers range. Hence, *unsigned int* may be a preferred type. Or *long*. In each case, be sure to adjust the print format in *printf()*. The second amendment to be proposed is the change of the function, from factori() to Fib(). This Fib() function returns the nth Fibonacci sequence element. Fibonacci, or Leonardo of Pisa, was the greatest European mathematician of the Middle Age and among his inventions there is the sequence that takes its name: 1, 1, 2, 3, 5, 8, 13, ... The building rule is: each term is the sum of the previous two. We have: Fib(1) = 1; Fib(2) = 1; Fib(3) = fib(2) + fib(1), ..., fib(n) = fib(n-1) + fib(n-2). In the *if* line the condition should include cases n = 1 and n = 2, which return Fib(n)=1. Therefore, the line begins with *if*(n= =1 || n= =2) ... In the next line, the term n*Factori(n-1) is replaced by the second member of the formula of Fib(n) above. A suggestion for the argument of the last *printf()* is '"\n Fib (%d)=%d", i, k '. The third proposed amendment is the introduction of a *for* before the 'k =' with a variable *j* (include it in the declaration) ranging from 1 to *i*, so that all values of the sequence, until it reaches the ith, are printed. In calling the Fib(), the argument should obviously be the variable *j*. And the argument of the *printf()* should be something like '"%d", k'.

Fast sorting

The Quicksort algorithm was developed by C. A. R. Hoare and published in 1962 (*Computer Journal*, paragraph 5, pp. 10-15). It is, today, the fastest method of ordering, numeric or alphanumeric, and has recursion on its strong point.

In C it looks like this:

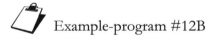 Example-program #12B

```
/* Program "Quicksor.cpp" */
    #include <stdio.h>
    #include <stdlib.h>
    #include <time.h>
    #define TOTAL 60
```

```
/*Quicksort Algorithm */
void Quicksort(int a[],int h,int r)
{ int i,j,x,t;
  i=h; j=r; x=a[(h+r)/2];
  do { while(a[i]<x) i++;
       while(x<a[j]) j--;
       if(i<=j) {t=a[i]; a[i]=a[j]; a[j]=t; i++; j--;}
     } while(i<=j);
     if(h<j) Quicksort(a,h,j);
     if(i<r) Quicksort(a,i,r);
}
main( )                      /* Array to sort */
{ int mat[TOTAL]; int i; srand(time(NULL));
  for(i=0;i<TOTAL;i++) mat[i]=rand();
  puts("\n Original array: "); for(i=0;i<TOTAL;i++)
  printf("%8d",mat[i]);
  Quicksort(mat,0,TOTAL-1);
  puts("\n Sorted array: "); for(i=0;i<TOTAL;i++)
  printf("%8d",mat[i]);
}
```

✐ Modifications to exercise: The first possible change is for the number of digits of the numbers generated to the array in *rand()*. To have smaller numbers you can make the division by 1000 of those that are generated in the current form, writing mat[i]=.001*rand(); in the line of the first *for*. Second amendment: change the number 8 in the *printf()* format to a smaller number of positions, finding what number will keep the arranged columns.

Selective sorting

For comparison, and cultural enrichment, the next example-program shows a more rudimentary algorithm, slower and more intuitive for ordination. There are several other similar processes, but it is sufficient, for our purposes here, to know the selective sorting algorithm

 Example-program #12C

```
/* Program "Selecsor.cpp" */
#include <stdio.h>
#include <stdlib.h>
#include <time.h>
#define TOTAL 60
int mat[TOTAL];
void Selectsort( )        /* Selectsort Algorithm */
{
   int i,j,k;
   for(i=0;i<TOTAL;i++)
   { k=i;
      for(j=i+1;j<TOTAL;j++) if(mat[j]<mat[k]) {
      int h=mat[k]; mat[k]=mat[j];mat[j]=h;}
   }
}
main( )                   /* Array to sort */
{
   int i; srand(time(NULL));
   for(i=0;i<TOTAL;i++) mat[i]=rand();
   puts("\n Original array: ");
   for(i=0;i<TOTAL;i++) printf("%8d",mat[i]);
   puts("\n Sorted array: ");
   Selectsort();
   for(i=0;i<TOTAL;i++) printf("%8d",mat[i]);
}
```

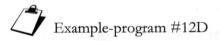 Modifications to exercise: The same amendments proposed to the previous program (Quicksor.cpp) can be experienced in Selectsor.cpp program.

Binary search

In the area of Data Structure many fine programming techniques are studied, including the linked allocation, storage of stacks and rows, the tree traversals (pre-order, in-order and post-order) and various processes of search in files. A rudimentary way to search is to compare the value you want with the values of the file in ascending order of indices. If the data are stored in the 1st index or records, the search will be fast, but if it is in a higher level, the research will be done in almost all file elements. On average, there is a number of at least n/2 comparisons for a file of *n* elements.

With the *binary search* algorithm the work optimizes the number of comparisons in the most productive imaginable way: the file is split down at the middle, by the average of its limit-indices; then the process is repeated on the left side or the right side, one that is not discarded in the comparison (for this, the file must be ordered). Continuing this operation, the sought datum (element) is found in the shortest possible time.

Example-program #12D

```
/* Program "Searchby.cpp" */
#include <stdio.h>
#include <stdlib.h>
#include <time.h>
#define TOTAL 60
int mat[TOTAL];
int Binarysearch(int element) /*Algorithm binary search */
```

```
{  int esq=0, dir=TOTAL-1, i;
   while(dir>=esq)   {i=(esq+dir)/2;
        if (element==mat[i]) return i;
        if (element < mat[i]) dir=i-1;
        else esq=i+1;}     return -1;
}
void Quicksort(int a[], int h, int r)
     /* Quicksort Algorithm */
{  int i,j,x,t; i=h;j=r;x=a[(h+r)/2];
   do
   {  while(a[i]<x)i++; while(x<a[j])j--;
        if(i<=j) {t=a[i];a[i]=a[j];a[j]=t;i++;j--;}
   }  while(i<=j);
   if(h<j) Quicksort(a,h,j);
   if(i<r) Quicksort(a,i,r);
}
int main( )                          /* Searching */
{ int i, element=0; srand(time(NULL)); /*Creating array*/
  for(i=0;i<TOTAL;i++) mat[i]=rand();
  puts("\n Matriz ordenada: ");   /* Sorting array */
  Quicksort(mat, 0, TOTAL-1);
  for(i=0;i<TOTAL;i++) printf("%8d",mat[i]);
  while(element!=-1)
  { puts("\n (Type -1 to exit ");  /* Searching element */
    printf("\n What value do you want find? ");
    scanf("%d",&element); fflush(stdin);
    if(elemento>=0) {i=Binarysearch(element);
       if (i>=0)
    printf("Pronto! mat[%d]=%d",i,mat[i]);
    else
    printf("\nArray doesn't contain the element %d",
       element);}
  }  return 0;
}
```

↩ Modifications to exercise: Again, the same amendments proposed in the two previous programs can be implemented.

Divide and conquer

The idea of splitting a set into two halves and, starting from there, to get to what you want is not exclusive of the *binary search* algorithm. It is the center of one of the most important techniques of programming: the technique of division and conquest (*divide and conquer*) transplanted from a famous strategy of the generals on the battlefield. When we separate the body of a program into modules, whether functions, whether procedures, we are using this famous technique.

On these algorithms presented just above, the reader needs to be reminded that the default file *stdlib.h* contains the *qsort()* (quick sort) and *bsearch()* (binary search) functions. They are algorithms important too much to get out of the standard library. And they are both too important to be not explicitly within this book, so that they can be manipulated by you, reader.

Flowchart

In the era of punch cards it was customary to draw the flow diagram, or flowchart, before writing a program. This was because the *goto* statement had everyday use, unlike what occurred later, and the major problems of involuntary interruption of flow or endless loop were the possible wrong use of that statement. The practice of avoiding it dismissed the use of the diagram, but you should know an example.

Let us look at a mini-program to add the square roots of the integers from 1 to 20.

```
#include <stdio.h>
#include <math.h>

main()
{      int i; float sum = 0;
       for (i = 1; i <= 20; i++) sum = sum + sqrt(i);
       printf ("\n The sum of the roots is s =% f", sum);
}
```

The flowchart of this program is represented by the diagram below.

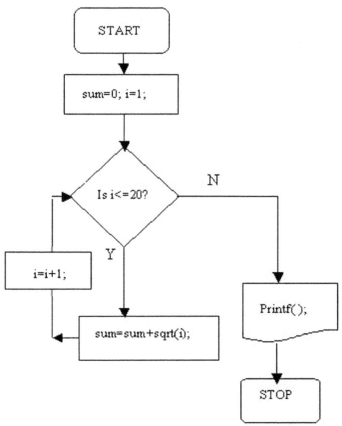

Exercises

1) Write a simple program that solves the absolute value equation of first degree $|a*x + b| = k$, with the parameters a, b and k, $k > 0$, data from the keyboard, with a being non-zero. Note that the resolution requires us to remove the expression in two first-degree equations without module: i) $a*x+b = -k$ and ii) $a*x+b = +k$.

2) Write a program that prints the symbol '@' in the first line once, on the second line twice, in the third row three times, and so on, until n times for a n number provided on the keyboard.

3) Create a program that receives temperature value in Celsius (C), convert it to Fahrenheit (F) and print it, knowing the $C/5 = (F-32)/9$ formula. It will be necessary, of course, isolate F.

4) Make a program that reads from the keyboard values of two cathetus, x and y, calculate the hypotenuse a, of the triangle, and also the sine and cosine of the angle formed by the first cathetus (of measurement x) with the hypotenuse (remembering that sine is y/a and cosine is x/a), printing these three results.

5) Write a program that prints on each line an integer random number of symbols '$' for a given number n of lines entered from the keyboard (see the last mini-program of Chapter 9 to manipulate the $rand()$ function).

6) Make a program that prints a table of values of mass and energy, using the equation of mass-energy equivalence, $E = mc^2$. The speed of light, c, is $3.0E+8$ m/s, so that c^2 is $9.0E+16$ m^2/s^2. The program should print ten lines after the header, indicating in the first column the mass, in kg, then the energy, in Joules (J), starting from a mass value m supplied via keyboard and iterated with 1 kg each, for example, if m = 16, the table shows the calculations for 16, 17, 18, ... 24.

7) Create a program for measuring population growth of bacteria, which is given by the exponential formula $N(t) = N_0 * r^{(t/d)}$. In this case, the growth rate, r = 2, and the doubling time, d = 5min,

are known. The formula then will be $N=N_0*2^{(t/5)}$. The program asks the user to provide from the keyboard the initial number N_0 of bacteria and the time t to wait, in minutes, to provide as a result the number N of bacteria.

8) Make a program that gives as a result the investment time t, in number of months, of an applying in compounds interest with a monthly rate r. The user must provide by the keyboard the rate r, the principal P and the desired amount A. The formula of compound interest is $A = P(1+r)^t$, from which we draw out t, by applying logarithms to both members of the equation, obtaining $log(A/P) = t*log(1+r)$ and, therefore, $t = log(A/P)/log(1+r)$.

9) We know that three non-collinear points determine a parabola, or quadratic equation. We can also determine a quadratic equation with only two points, with different ordinates, one of these points being the vertex. This is even easier when the other point is the ordinate of zero, or intercept, (0, c). What is required here from the reader is to build a program that gives as a result the quadratic equation $y=a*x^2+b*x+c$, with the value of the intercept, c, and x_v and y_v coordinates of vertex given from the keyboard, knowing that $x_V = -b/(2*a)$ and $y_V = -(b^2-4*a*c)/(4*a)$. Since the value of c is already provided, we only need to calculate a and b (just isolate a in x_v and replace the value in y_v, for obtaining b).

10) Develop a program that calculates the sequence of prime numbers up to a given integer n, obtained from the keyboard. Prime number is one that has exactly two divisors, it and the unit. Note that the test within the program does not need to divide by an integer greater than the square root of n, once, if greater, the other number of the factor will be smaller and has been already tested, assuming that you are testing these numbers in ascending order.

11) Create a program that calculates the least common multiple (LCM) of two integers n and p, given via the keyboard. The two integers must be divided by the result of the prime numbers, in ascending order, repeating the operation with the quotients, until both quotients are the unit. If, for a given prime number, one is

CACILDO MARQUES

divisible and the other is not, the one that is not divisible remains, as if it were quotient. The product of the successful prime numbers in the divisions, those that have had remainder zero, it will be the LCM.

12) When developing your program to calculate the numbers of Bernoulli, the first program in history, Ada Byron realized that, from the series shown first in the formulas with the sum below, she could isolate the values B_n, as shown in the second formula, II, which are the Bernoulli numbers. The challenge here is to build a program that calculates and prints the result of these numbers up to a given value, for example n = 10, i. e., the numbers B_0, B_1, B_2, B_3, ... B_{10}, starting from $B_0 = 1$. The reader should not be surprised that the even index numbers, after B_2, are all null, because that is the nature of the sequence. The results should be in fraction form, as the default for this sequence, and the Ada formula, by the way, already has a denominator n+1. We should recall that the number of combinations of *m* elements taken *k* at a time is given by $\binom{m}{k} =$

$\frac{m!}{k!(n-k)!}$ and, thus, $\binom{n+1}{k} = \frac{(n+1)!}{k!(n+1-k)!}$. You can make use of the factorial function, of the example-program #13A, but may find it more appropriate to use something simpler, given that combination of *m* elements taken k at a time is the product operator of m-i, *i* from zero to k-1, divided by the product operator of k-i, *i* from zero to k-1. Ada says that, by limitation of the machine, she omitted the negative sign before the B_n formula. With the current machines we can work with sign, changing the value 1 of the numerator by -1. You will need to build also a small routine to add and, with the HCF (example-program #9B), to simplify the fractions that appear as a result.

(I) $\dfrac{x}{e^x - 1} = \sum_{n=0}^{\infty} \dfrac{B_n}{n!}$ (II) $B_n = \dfrac{1}{n+1}\sum_{k=0}^{n-1}\binom{n+1}{k}B_k$

90

APPENDIX A
Examples with reserved words

This section presents mini-programs for 32 reserved words in ANSI C. They all need to be started with the *#include <stdio.h>*, at least.

auto
```
void Algar() {auto int i; for(i=0;i<10;i++) printf(" %d",i);}
main() {Algar();}
```

break
```
main() {char c;int i; for(i=1;i<=1000;i++){c=getchar();
      if(c=='\n') break; else printf("\a");}}
```

case
```
main() {char c; puts("\n Type uppercase vowel: ");
      c=getchar();switch(c) {case'A':puts("Ann");break;
      case'E': puts("Eve");break;case'I':puts("Ivy");break;
      default: puts("O, U, Y ou Error.");}}
```

char
```
main() {int i,j;char k[20],n[20];puts(" Tyoe number:");
      gets(k);puts("Other: ");gets(n);i=atoi(k);j=atoi(n);
      printf("\n%d  %d",div(i,j));}
```

const   (rem.: with *math.h*)
```
main() {float x;const float pi=3.14159;x=pi/4;
      printf("\ncos(%f)=%f",x,cos(x));}
```

continue
```
main() {int k;while(k<10){
    puts("\n Type number lower than 10 (greater to exit): ");
    scanf("%d",&k);printf(" Square: %d",k*k);  if(k>1) continue;
```

}}

default
```
main() {int n; puts("\n Press even digit: ");
    scanf("%d",&n); switch(n) {case 0: puts("Zero.");break;
    case 2: puts("Two."); break; default:
    puts("Greater than 3, or Error.");}}
```

do
```
main() {int k,i=1; puts(" Press odd number: ");
    scanf("%d",&k); do{printf(" %d",i);i+=2;} while(i<=k);}
```

double
```
main() {double x; float t=1.256; x=tan(t);
    printf("\ntan(%f)=%f",t,x);}
```

else
```
main() {int k; srand(time(NULL)); k=rand(); if(k<16383)
    printf("\nLower."); else printf("\nGreater.");}
```

enum
```
main() {enum Elem{water,fire,earth=5,air}; int i;
    enum Elem subs;subs=fire;i=subs+1;
    printf("\nFire: %d, Fire+1: %d, Air: %d.",subs,i,air);}
```

extern
```
int Q(k){k=k*k; return k;}
main(){extern int k; int n;   puts("\nType number:");
    scanf("\n %d",&n);printf("\n Q=%d",Q(n));}
```

float
```
main() {float t,v;srand(time(NULL));v=rand();t=v/32767;
    printf("\nProbab=%f",t);}
```

for

```
main() {char c; int i,n; puts("\nType multiple of 5: ");
    scanf("%d",&n); for(i=0;i<=n;i+=5) printf(" %d",i);}
```

goto

```
main() {char c; puts("Type something ('e' to exit): ");
    REDO: c=getchar();putchar(c); if(c!='p') goto REDO;}
```

if

```
main() {if('a'<'b') printf("\n
I can compare characters by ASCII value. Ex: a<b.");}
```

int

```
int main() {int i; for(i=60;i>0;i--)printf(" %d",i);}
```

long

```
main() {long n; int i; for(i=0;i<=5000;i+=25){n=10*i;
    printf("%d ",n);}}
```

register   (obs.: with math.h)

```
main() {register k; float y; for(k=0;k<41;k++) {
    y=sqrt(k); printf("   %d %1.1f",k,y);}}
```

return

```
long Cube(int n){return n*n*n;}
main() {int k; puts("\nType number:");
    scanf("%d",&k); printf("%d",Cube(k));}
```

short

```
main(){short m;float j,k;puts("\nType two numbers:");
scanf("%f %f",&j,&k); m=fmod(j,k);
printf("\nRemainder: %d",m);}
```

signed

```
main() {signed int i;
    puts("\n"); for(i=-20;i<=20;i+=2) printf(" %d",i);}
```

sizeof
```
main() {float a,e=2.71828; a=100*e;
    printf("\nValor: %f Bytes: %d",a,sizeof(float));}
```

static (rem.: with *math.h*)
```
main(){static float t,y;puts("\nType positive number:");
    scanf("%f",&y); t=cos(3.14/6); t=log 10(t);
    printf("\nL=%f log(cos(pi/4))=%f",log10(y),t);}
```

struct (rem.: with string.h)
```
main() {struct Cla{char mt[30];float m;}; struct Cla ja;
    strcpy(ja.mt,"Tue"); ja.m=5.7;
    printf("\nSubject: %s\nMark: %2.1f",ja.mt,ja.m);}
```

switch
```
main() {char c; puts("\nMarried?(y/n): "); c=getchar();
    switch(c) {case's': puts("Spouse.");break; case'n':
    puts("Single."); break, default:puts("Error!");}}
```

typedef
```
typedef enum Boole{fals, true}Boole;
main() {Boole ini; ini=true; printf("\n Value=%d",ini);}
```

union
```
main() {union Some{char k; int i;}asc;
    puts("\nType character:\n ");asc.k=getchar();asc.i=asc.k;
    printf("%d %c Number: %d\n", asc.k, asc.k, asc.i);}
```

unsigned (rem.: with *math.h*)
```
main() {unsigned int n;n=fabs(floor(log10(.005)));
    printf("\n abs(log(x))=%d",n);}
```

void

```
void Answer(){printf("\nDisobedient!");}
main() {char j;puts("\nType anything, except '*':");
    j=getchar();if(j!='*') printf("\nAsc %d",j); else Answer();}
```

volatile

```
main() {volatile float u,x=0; puts("\n Type positive value");
    scanf("\n %f",&x);
    for(u=1;u<=x;u++) printf("\n %.1f",u/2);}
```

while

```
main() {char c;puts("\nType character:");
    do{scanf("\n %c",&c);printf("\nCode: %d\n('!' finish)\n\n",c);}
    while(c!='!');}
```

APPENDIX B
List of library functions in C and C++

The functions contained in the various header files of the standard library, and those of the *conio.h* file are shown below together with their syntax, their location and their meaning.

Function	Syntax	Header	Meaning
abort()	void abort(void);	stdlib.h	by error output
abs()	int abs(int k);	stdlib.h	absolute value
acos()	double acos(double x);	math.h	arc cosine
asctime()	char *asctime(const struct tm *pthora);	time.h	time string
asin()	double asin(double x);	math.h	arc sine
assert()	void assert(sentence);	assert.h	T-F test
atan()	double atan(double x);	math.h	arctangent
atan2()	double atan(double y, double x);	math.h	arc tangent with cathetus
atexit()	int atexit(void(*funct) (void))	stdlib.h	registration of functions
atof()	double atof(const char *s);	stdlib.h	conversion to float
atoi()	int atoi(const char *s);	stdlib.h	conversion to int
atol()	long int atol(const char *s);	stdlib.h	conversion to long

bsearch()	*void *bsearch(const void *key, const void *base, size_t n,size_t size, int(*comp)(const void*, const void *));*	*stdlib.h*	binary search
calloc()	*void *calloc(size_t* n, *size_t* size);	*stdlib.h*	creating memory
ceil()	*double ceil(double* x);	*math.h*	entire ceiling
cgets()	*char *cgets(char **s);	*conio.h*	string keyboard
clearerr()	*void clearerr(FILE *flow);*	*stdio.h*	zero error condition
clock()	*clock_t clock(void);*	*time.h*	processing time
cos()	*double cos(double* x);	*math.h*	cosine
cosh()	*double(cosh(double* x);	*math.h*	hyperbolic cosine
cputs()	*int cputs(const char *s);*	*conio.h*	Video for output
cprintf()	*int cprintf(const* char format,...);	*conio.h*	formatted output in vídeo
cscanf()	*int cscanf(const char *format,...);*	*conio.h*	keyboard data
ctime()	*char *ctime(const time_t *pthor);*	*time.h*	time string
div()	*div_t div(int* numer, *int* denom);	*stdlib.h*	quotient eresto
difftime()	*double difftime(time_t hor1, time_thor2);*	*time.h*	timepieces difference
exit()	*void exit(int* n);	*stdlib.h*	by error output
exp()	*double exp(double* x);	*math.h*	exponential ex
fabs()	*double fabs(double* x);	*ath.h*	absolute value
fclose()	*int fclose(FILE *flw);*	*tdio.h*	close file
feof()	*int feof(FILE *flw);*	*stdio.h*	of fimde test file

ferror()	int ferror(FILE *flw);	tdio.h	test fluxopara error
fflush()	int fflush(FILE *flw);	stdio.h	file recording and buffer cleaning
fgetc()	int fgetc(FILE *flw);	tdio.h	character reading
fgetpos()	FILE fgetpos(FILE *flw, fpos_t*pos);	tdio.h	position indicator
fgets()	char *fgets(char*s, int n, FILE *flw);	tdio.h	n-1 characters read
floor()	double floor(double x);	ath.h	entire floor
fmod()	double fmod(double x, double n);	ath.h	congruence module n
fopen()	FILE *fopen(const char *file, const char *mode);	tdio.h	file open
fprintf()	int fprintf(FILE *flw, const char format,...);	stdio.h	File print
fputc()	int fputc(int c, FILE *flw);	stdio.h	character recording
fputs()	int fputs(const char *s, FILE *flw);	stdio.h	recording string
fread()	size_t fread(void*pt, size_t tam, size_t n, FILE *flx);	stdio.h	reading n elements
free()	void free(void*pt);	stdlib.h	allocation of memory
freopen()	FILE *freopen(const char *file, const char *mode, FILE *flw);	stdio.h	replacement flow
frexp()	double frexp(double x, int *n);	math.h	mantissa m with m = n-x.2

fscanf()	*int fscanf(*FILE *flw, *const char*format,...);*	*stdio.h*	formatted input
fseek()	*int fseek(*FILE *flw, *long int* desloc, *int since);*	*stdio.h*	positioning indicator
fsetpos()	*int fsetpos(*FILE *flw, *const fpos_t* *pos);*	*stdio.h*	positioning pos *
ftell()	*long int ftell(*FILE *flw);*	*stdio.h*	positioning from zero
fwrite()	*size_t fwrite(const void *pt, size_t tam,size_t n, FILE *flw);*	*stdio.h*	writing to the file
getc()	*int getc(*FILE *flw);*	*stdio.h*	reading characters
getch()	*int getch(void);*	*conio.h*	reading characters
getchar()	*int getchar(void)*	*stdio.h*	reading characters
getche()	*int getche(void)*	*conio.h*	reading characters
getenv()	*char *getenv(const char *name);*	*stdlib.h*	environmental information
gets()	*char *gets(char *s);*	*stdio.h*	string read
gmtime()	*struct tm * gmtime(const time_t *hor);*	*time.h*	Greenwich Mean Time
inp()	*int inp(int* n);*	*conio.h*	door byte
isalnum	*int isalnum(int* c);*	*ctype.h*	character test (A-Z, a-z, 0-9)
isalpha()	*int isalpha(int* c);*	*ctype.h*	test (A-Z, a-z)
iscntrl()	*int iscntrl(int* c);*	*ctype.h*	test (0-31 or 127)
isdigit()	*int isdigit(int* c);*	*ctype.h*	test (0-9)
isgraph()	*ins isgraph(int* c);*	*ctype.h*	test (minus 32)
islower()	*int islower(int* c);*	*ctype.h*	test (a-z)
isprint()	*int isprint(int* c);*	*ctype.h*	test (32-126)

ispunct()	*int ispunct(int c);*	*ctype.h*	test (32-47,58-63, 91-96,123-126)
isspace()	*int isspace(int c);*	*ctype.h*	teste (se espaço)
isupper()	*int isupper(int c);*	*ctype.h*	teste (A-Z)
isxdigit()	*int isxdigit(int c);*	*ctype.h*	teste (0-9,A-F,a-f)
kbhit()	*int kbhit(void);*	*conio.h*	character test (if available)
labs()	*long int labs(long int n);*	*stdlib.h*	absolute value
ldexp()	*double ldexp(double m, double n);*	*math.h*	value of $m.2^n$
ldiv()	*ldiv_t ldiv(long int num, long int denom);*	*stdlib.h*	quotient and remainder
localtime()	*struct tm localtime(const time_t *hour);*	*time.h*	local time
log()	*double log(double x);*	*math.h*	natural logarithm
log10()	*double log10(double x);*	*math.h*	logarithm
longjmp()	*void longjmp(jmp_buf env, int n);*	*setjmp.h*	no local detour
malloc()	*void *malloc(size_t size);*	*stdlib.h*	Memory Allocation
mblen()	*int mblen(const *char*s, size_t n);*	*stdlib.h*	amount of bytes
mbstowcs()	*size_t mbstowcs(wchar_t *pw, const char *s, int n);*	*stdlib.h*	conversion bytes
mbtowc()	*int mbtowc(wchar_t const char *s, size_t n);*	*stdlib.h*	amount of bytes
memchr()	*void *memchr(const void *s, int c size_t n);*	*string.h*	Location characters

memcmp()	int memcmp(const unsigned char *s1, const unsigned char *s2, size_t n);	string.h	comparing characters
memcpy()	void memcpy(void *s1, void *s2, size_t n);	string.h	print character
memmove()	void *memmove(void *s1, const void *s2, size_t n);	string.h	move n characters
memset()	void *memset(void *s, int c; size_t n);	string.h	propagation of c, n times
mktime()	time_t mktime(struct tm *pthour);	time.h	calendar
modf()	double modf(double x, double *py);	math.h	fractional part of byte
outp()	int outp(int p, int b);	conio.h	Prom output per port
perror()	void perror(const char *s);	stdio.h	error message
printf()	int printf(const char *format,...);	stdio.h	print formatted
pow()	double pow(double x, double y);	math.h	power xy
putc()	int putc(int c, FILE *flw);	stdio.h	character recording
putch()	int putch(int c);	conio.h	c display
putchar()	int putchar(int c);	stdio.h	c writing to stdout
puts()	int puts(const char *s);	stdio.h	s write to stdout
qsort()	void qsort(void *base, size_t n, size_t size, int(*fcmp) (const void *, const void *);	stdlib.h	fast sorting

raise()	*int raise(int* n*);*	*signal.h*	error condition signal
rand()	*int rand(void)*	*stdlib.h*	Random number generator
realloc()	*void realloc(void* *pt, *size_t size);*	*stdlib.h*	memory reallocation
remove()	*int remove(const char *file);*	*stdio.h*	file deletion
rename()	*int rename(const char *old, const char *new);*	*stdio.h*	file renaming
rewind()	*void rewind(*FILE *lw*);*	*stdio.h*	"Rewind" from the beginning
scanf()	*int scanf(const char *format,...);*	*stdio.h*	formatted reading
setbuf()	*void setbuf(*FILE *lw*);*	*stdio.h*	specification beating
setjmp()	*int setjmp(jmp_buf env);*	*setjmp.h*	environment storage
setvbuf()	*int setvbuf(*FILE *lw, *buf, *int mode, size_t size);*	*stdio.h*	establishment beating
signal()	*void *signal(int* sig, *void(func)(int));*	*signal.h*	treatment signal
sin()	*double sin(double* x*);*	*math.h*	sine
sinh()	*double sinh(double* x*);*	*math.h*	hyperbolic sine
sprintf()	*int sprintf(char* *s, *const char *format,...);*	*stdio.h*	formatted print
srand()	*void srand(unsigned int seede);*	*stidlib.h*	random initialization
sqrt()	*double sqrt(double* x*);*	*math.h*	square root

sscanf()	int sscanf(const char *s, const char *format,...);	stdio.h	formatted input
strcat()	char *strcat(char *s1, const char *s2);	string.h	string concatenation
strchr()	char *strchr(const char *s, int c);	string.h	search string s
strcmp()	int strcmp(const unsigned char *s1, const unsigned char *s2);	string.h	Destrings comparison
strcoll()	int strcoll(const char *s1,const char *s2);	string.h	comparison local strings
strcpy()	char *strcpy(char *s1, const char *s2);	string.h	copy strings
strcspn()	int strcspn(const char *s1,const char *s2);	string.h	number of characters in s1 not in s2
strerror()	char strerror(int num);	string.h	error message
strftime()	size_t strftime(char *s, size_t size, const char *format,...);	time.h	string time
strlen()	int strlen(const char *s);	string.h	string size
strncat()	char *strncat(char *s1, const char *s2, size_t n);	string.h	string concatenation
strncmp()	int strncmp(const unsigned char *s1, const unsigned char *s2, size_t n);	string.h	string comparison
strncpy()	char strncpy(char *s1, const char *s2,	string.h	copy strings

strpbrk()	char *strpbrk(const char *s1, const char *s2);	string.h	search string (last)
strrchr()	char *strrchr(const char *s, int c);	string.h	search character
strspn()	size_t strspn(const char *s, int c);	string.h	character count
strstr()	char *strstr(const char *s1, const char *s2);	string.h	substring search
strtod()	double strtod(const char *pt, char **pf);	stdlib.h	conversion to double
strtok()	char *strtok(char *s1, const char *s2);	string.h	string break
strtol()	long int strtol(const char *pt, char **pf, int base);	stdlib.h	conversion to long
strtoul()	unsigned long int strtoul(const char *pt, char **pf, int base);	stdlib.h	conversion to unsigned long
strxfrm()	size_t strxfrm(char *s1, const char *s2, size_t n);	string.h	string processing
system()	int system(const char *s);	stdlib.h	string transfer
tan()	double tan(double x);	math.h	tangent
tanh()	double tanh(double x);	math.h	hyperbolic tangent
time()	time_t time(time_t *pthour);	time.h	hour
tmpfile()	FILE *tmpfile(void)	stdio.h	open temporary file
tmpnam()	char *tmpnam(char *s);	stdio.h	appoint temporary file
tolower()	int tolower(int c);	ctype.h	tiny for conversion

toupper()	*int toupper(int* c *);*	*ctype.h*	conversion to uppercase
ungetc()	*int ungetc(int* c, *FILE *flw);*	*stdio.h ou conio.h*	character return
va_arg()	*void va_arg(*lis_prm, *ult_par);*	*stdarg.h*	pointing advance
va_end()	*void va_end(*lis_prm *);*	*stdarg.h*	end of va_arg ()
va_start()	*void va_start(*lis_prm, *prm_n);*	*stdarg.h*	cell start indication
vfprintf()	*int vprintf(char **s, *const char *format,args);*	*stdio.h*	formatted print
vprintf()	*int vprintf(const char *format,args);*	*stdio.h*	formatted print
vsprintf()	*int vsprintf(char **s, *const char *format, args);*	*stdio.h*	formatted print
wcstombs()	*size_t wcstombs(char *s, const wchar_t *pw, size_t n);*	*stdlib.h*	character storage
wcstomb()	*size_t wcstomb(char *s, wchar_t wchar);*	*stdlib.h*	character storage

APPENDIX C
Binary arithmetic: bits and bytes

The ENIAC computer, built at the Pennsylvania State University in 1945, already used binary arithmetic as base of its architecture. This arithmetic admits only two digits, zero and one (hence the name), and was invented by Leibniz, who invented also the multiplication machine.

The representation within the computer is given as follows: Circuit ON corresponds to the number 1; circuit OFF corresponds to the number zero.

As there is no other digit greater than 1, all numbers besides 2 are written with the use of two or more digits.

We have:

1	1	10
+0	+1	+1
1 (for 1)	10 (for 2)	11 (for 3)

and so on. Whenever we add 1+1, the result is zero and 1 "goes up", such as in base 10 when we add 9+1, since 9 is the last digit of that base.

Each space to be occupied by a binary digit is called a bit (contraction of "binary digit"), word created for this purpose, by Professor Claude Shannon, of MIT (Massachusetts Institute of Technology).

Each sequence of eight bits form one "byte".

Representation of a byte:

|↑|↓|↑|↑|↓|↓|↑|↓|

In binary digits:

|1 |0 |1 |1 |0 |0 |1 |0 |

To convert to the base 10:

$10110010_{(2)} = 1*2^7 + 0*2^6 + 1*2^5 + 1*2^4 + 0*2^3 + 0*2^2 + 1*2 + 0*2 =$

$= 2^7 + 2^5 + 2^4 + 2 = 178.$

(This is the so-called polynomial notation of number. In powers of ten, the polynomial notation would be $178 = 1*10^2 + 7*10 + 8$.)

To turn the base ten to binary base we divide the number by two and took the remainder (the first time gives the unit). We repeat the process for transforming the quotient in dividend, until the quotient is zero. (Of course, the machine does it for us, but it is not comfortable to ignore such a simple process.)

Example: Write 300 in base two.

```
300 |2     150 |2     75 |2     37 |2     18 |2     9 |2    4 |2
 10 150     10 75     15 37     17 18      0 9      1 4     0 2
  0           0         1         1
                                 2 |2      1 |2    .
                                  0 1       1 0
 ↑                                 ↑ first digit (remainder)
```

(last digit – the unit)

The number 300 is written in binary base as $100101100_{(2)}$.

Another example: Write 57 in base two.

```
57|2    28|2    14|2    7|2    3|2    1|2
17 28   08 14    0 7    1 3    1 1    1 0
 1       0                             ↑
```

We have: $57 = 111001_{(2)}$ first digit

If we type a letter (alphanumeric character), this character is immediately associated with a number, the ASCII code, and this is transformed into binary base number. In microcomputers we have the ASCII, but the old mainframe code used is EBCDIC.

Eight-bit computers are those whose architecture allows you to process information in eight by eight bits. Those of 16 bits do it in

16 by 16 and so on.

Eight bits: MSX, Apple, etc.
16 bits: IBM-PC, Amiga, etc.
32 bits: IBM PC-AT 386DX, IBM PC-AT 486DX, etc.
64 bits: IBM PS1, Pentium, etc.

Hexadecimal numerals

The base 16, or hexadecimal base, is widely used in computing because of space and time saving, since in it numbers are written with fewer symbols and the transition to the binary base is faster than in decimal numerals.

The figures are: 0, 1, 2, 3, 4, 5, 6, 7, 8, 9, A, B, C, D, E and F, with $A = 10$, $B = 11$, etc.

Let's convert 1039 into base 16.

```
1039|16      64|16      4|16
079 64        0 4       4  0
 15
   ↑ F: unit
```

We have: $1039 = h40F$. (The "h" is the initial of hexadecimal.)

Today it is more common to use $0x40F$ ("0x" is the notation in C language).

Let us now turn a 16 base number to base ten, for example, the number $0xDE2$.

$0xDE2 = 13*16^2 + 14*16^1 + 2*16^0 = 13*256 + 14*16 + 2*1 = 3554$.

(Note that $D=13$ and $E=14$.)

Binary to hexadecimal

The number 16 is the fourth power of 2, i. e., $16 = 2^4$, for this motive, four digits of a binary number result in a figure of base 16 of a digit.

Here is an example:

00010001

    1   1

We have: $00010001_{(2)} = 11_{(16)}$. (It is the number 17 in base ten.)

More examples:

a) 01000011.......$01000011_{(2)} = 43_{(16)}$

     4 2+1

b) 11000101.......$11000101_{(2)} = C5_{(16)}$

     8+4 4+1

c) 10100111.......$10100111_{(2)} = A8_{(16)}$

     8+2 4+2+1

d) 10001110.......$10001110_{(2)} = 8E_{(16)}$

     8 8+4+2

Hexadecimal to binary

To transform the base 16 to base two is sufficient to remember that each hexadecimal digit results in four binary digits, and then transform each one in four orders.

Example: Turning 0xBC5 in binary number.

$B_{(16)} = 11$ 11|2   5|2   2|2   1|2 $B_{(16)} = 1011_{(2)}$

               1 5   1 2   0 1   1 0

$C_{(16)} = 12$ 12|2   6|2   3|2   1|2 $C_{(16)} = 1100_{(2)}$

               0 6   0 3   1 1   1 0

$5(16) = 5$ 5|2   2|2   1|2 $5_{(16)} = 0101_{(2)}$

               1 2   0 1   1 0

We have: $BC5_{(16)} = 101111000101_{(2)}$.

Remark: The octal base is also important, but not as much as the binary and hexadecimal ones. The handling is similar to that of the latter.

Exercises

E41. Write in base ten the following numbers:
   a) $101110_{(2)}$ b) $11001101_{(2)}$ c) $10000100_{(2)}$ c) $110_{(2)}$
E42. Write in base 2 the following numbers:
   a) 56 b) 1000 c) 450 d) 1024
E43. Write in hexadecimal:
   a) 250 b) 1128 c) 256 d) 4000
E44. Write in polynomial notation:
   a) 1250 b) 323 c) 45 871 d) 510
E45. Write in base ten:
   a) 0xE8 b) 0xAB5 c) 0xAAB d) 0xFA
E46. Write in hexadecimal:
   a) $1110_{(2)}$ b) $10000100_{(2)}$ c) $10110_{(2)}$ d) $11100011_{(2)}$
E47. Write in binary basis:
   a) 0xC8 b) 0xFA c) 0x7E d) 0x99

@cacildo

www.ingramcontent.com/pod-product-compliance
Lightning Source LLC
Chambersburg PA
CBHW071004050326
40689CB00014B/3485